LIVING F

LIVING
FOR GOD
in the modern world

by

John Grant

JOHN RITCHIE LTD
CHRISTIAN PUBLICATIONS

40 Beansburn, Kilmarnock, Scotland

ISBN-13: 978 0 946351 43 5
ISBN-10: 0 946351 43 0

Copyright © 2009 by John Ritchie Ltd.
40 Beansburn, Kilmarnock, Scotland

www.ritchiechristianmedia.co.uk

Typeset by John Ritchie Ltd., Kilmarnock
Printed by Bell & Bain Ltd., Glasgow

Contents

Foreword

Each generation will read and interpret the Scriptures against the background of the spiritual and social climate of its own age. It is a clear evidence of divine inspiration that the Word of God has a relevant message for our day. It can answer the problems which arise in our minds; it can instruct us on how to live for God.

Most of the chapters of this book originally appeared as articles in the *Believer's Magazine* over a period of 19 months. The material within them covers a wide spectrum of important issues which, from the early stages of spiritual development, confront every believer in the Lord Jesus Christ. Each subject has been dealt with in a clear and honest manner, and frequent reference has been made to Scripture to give support to the teaching given.

Mr Grant has approached each subject as an answer to a particular question which can arise within the mind of the reader. The sequence of the questions considered is orderly, from initial salvation with its immediate requirements, through to many practical aspects of Christian living, including such matters as employment, social life, politics, courtship, and marriage.

Travelling in various parts, the present writer has heard appreciation expressed, and a desire for this written ministry to be put in permanent form. It is therefore good that the publishers have made it available to a wider readership. It is heartily commended to all; we are sure it will prove a blessing and help to those who read it.

J R Baker

Introduction

The substance of this small book is made up of articles which appeared in the "Young Believers Page" of the *Believer's Magazine* from late 1991 until mid 1993. The purpose of the articles was to bring before young believers some topical issues which are vital to those who are seeking to live for God.

Four additional chapters have been added and some other small changes made, but, in the main, the material has been left in the form in which it appeared. Each chapter, therefore, suffers from the constraints on length to which magazine articles are subject. It does not claim to be an exhaustive study of each topic, but merely a suggestive outline which can be read quickly.

The book goes forth with the prayer that it may help some to realise the privilege and joy which are the experience of all who have a genuine desire to live for God.

Bridge of Weir, September 1994

CHAPTER 1

Saved! Now what?

So you are saved! You have accepted Christ as your Lord and Saviour and are eager to know what His will is for your life and what you have to do to make sure that you serve Him and live in fellowship with Him.

How important it is that we treat this subject seriously. We have only one life to live and we shall have no opportunity of re-living wasted years. Some people seem to think that living for God is only for those who are older, and that it leads to a life where we are constantly saying "No" to everything that brings joy and happiness; a stern disciplined life that must be tolerated if we are to get to heaven.

What a misconception this is! God's salvation gives us a life that is fuller and more rewarding than that which is experienced by those who never know the Saviour. Remember that the message of the gospel has "promise of the life that now is, and of that which is to come" (1 Tim 4.8). It is not necessary to wait until eternity before enjoying God and salvation. It can start now.

This will not happen without effort on our part. Should we neglect our spiritual life we shall never realise its full potential, and we shall become believers who are going to heaven, but who are either too immature to serve intelligently, or have been disapproved for service by conduct that does not correspond to the Word of God (1 Cor 9.27). Our lives will be of such a character that we will not be permitted, and probably will not have the desire, to carry out useful service for God.

'But", you may ask, "if we are all going to heaven, does this really matter? Can we not live here as we please, knowing that we have eternal life no matter what we do with the years which we are given?"

Do we also sometimes find the thought crossing our minds that the Bible was suitable for a society of two thousand years ago, but it cannot meet the needs or relate to the problems of today? Can the teaching of the Bible be put into practice now, and, even if it can, does the life which results have any real benefits over a life lived to enjoy the world to the full? Is it even possible to get the best of both worlds? Can we be saved and yet miss nothing of the apparent excitement and attraction which those of our friends who have no interest in spiritual things seem to enjoy?

The chapters that follow examine these questions, and address some of the current challenges and difficulties faced by young believers. We will discover that striving to please God in everything is the secret of a satisfying life. The challenge to us is whether we are prepared to allow Him to direct our lives, or whether we prefer to drift through life, never, other than in salvation, experiencing the hand of God with us, and content that our knowledge of Him should be what others tell us. We would then only experience second-hand Christianity. Surely we would wish to have more than that!

What resources then do we have as we commence this endeavour of living for God? If it is His desire for us to live in a way that pleases Him, surely there must be means at our disposal to make this possible? Indeed, there are! First, we have eternal life. This is not merely an existence that will be forever. Those who are not believers will also exist forever, so in the gospel when we learn that we have eternal life it must indicate something much greater than unending existence.

The expression "eternal life" denotes the quality of the life that God gave us when we accepted the Lord Jesus Christ as our Saviour, and we can never lose it (Jn 10.28). Those who have eternal life will never suffer the judgment of God for their sins. It is the life which has to do with future glory, and yet God in His grace has given us this now. Because we have this life we have come to know God (Jn 17.3); unlike the unbeliever we have the love of God in us (Jn 5.42), we enjoy His peace (Jn 16.33), and we know His joy (Jn 17.13). Surely we see from this that eternal life is never dull or humdrum. It is life to be lived to the full.

Second, one of the most amazing results of salvation is that we now have the Holy Spirit. When we were saved the Holy Spirit came to dwell within us (Jn 14.17). He is the source of power in living for God. This truth compels us to be careful in how we use our bodies. He is indwelling us and, although we can never expel Him, we can grieve Him by our conduct (Eph 4.30).

In addition to these two great resources, we also have the Word of God. What a book this is, fulfilling its role as an unending source of instruction to all who seek to live for God. If we study it systematically we will find that the Scriptures live, and every page will be of absorbing interest. If we pay them scant attention we will find that we miss the very best which God has for us and that the Bible is of little interest to us. We ignore the Scriptures at our peril. Without them we will never progress in spiritual life.

With the Scriptures before us we have the answers to the problems which puzzle others so much. When men say that they do not know what the world is coming to they are expressing their concern at an unknown future, faced with some trepidation. As believers, however, we do know what the world is coming to, and we also know what it has come from and why it is as it is today.

But in addition to all these blessings we must not forget that we also have the work of the Lord Jesus Christ presently for us. The work of redemption was completed at the cross, but His work for His own did not stop there. He is our Great High Priest with God and appears in His presence continually for us. He is our Advocate with the Father, and when we seek to pursue a godly life, but find ourselves sinning, He ensures that our communion with the Father is restored. We must, through the study of the Scriptures, come to understand what He has done, what He is doing presently, and what He will yet do on our behalf.

These are just a few of the many resources which we have at our disposal. The question facing us now is, "How serious are we in our desire to live for God?". If we are determined to go in for this life, the best to be had, and to devote our years to Him, He has promised that He will reveal His truth to us and that we shall see His hand guiding, comforting, and helping us in so many ways. We shall have our own precious memories of God working in our lives. What a life that will be, but are we prepared to go in for it?

The Lord Jesus on one occasion was met by three men, two of whom claimed to want to become disciples (Lk 9.57-62). Two of these men expressed their desires very forcibly in His presence. One asserted, "Lord, I will follow thee whithersoever thou goest"; the third stated, "Lord, I will follow thee; but let me first go bid them farewell which are at home at my house". The second was different from the other two. There is no record of him making the claim, "I will follow thee", but in response to the call of the Lord Jesus to follow Him he exclaimed, "Lord, suffer me first to go and bury my father".

If you seek to follow the Lord Jesus you do well to consider these three. The first was a man of an impetuous nature. He doubtless had seen the Lord at work and observed the crowds who followed Him. It appeared that being a disciple was a pathway to a good lifestyle, and the excitement of it all overwhelmed him so that, without calm consideration, he made his great claim. Christian life must not be approached in this way. It is not a case of excitement and a crowded diary. It is not an alternative way of life which will always be lived on a "high". No! This life must be approached soberly with consideration of the claims made by the Lord on those who follow Him and the numberless blessings which He has promised those who devote their lives to Him. The answer of the Lord to this man is telling. He emphasises the sacrifice which His followers must make by saying, "Foxes have holes, birds of the air have nests; but the Son of man hath not where to lay his head". Sacrifices have to be made by those who seek to serve Him. The problem with this would-be disciple was that he wished to have comfort rather than consecration.

The third man said he would come, but only after he had gone home to bid farewell to his family. This was a weak excuse and the mark of a man who was irresolute. He would serve, but have his usefulness diminished by the constant pull of that which, although legitimate, had to be sacrificed in following Him. The Lord did not suggest, therefore, that discipleship is an easy pathway; He stated on more than one occasion that it is demanding and can be difficult, but immensely rewarding. The servant of God must be dedicated to His calling and not easily turned aside from His pathway. This man illustrated in his request that it is possible to let the company of family and friends come before Him.

Do you note that the Lord called neither of these; He did not say to them, "Follow me". The second man, however, heard that call and responded by asking that he first go and bury his father. The burial of his father was a responsibility which he would not evade, but it appears that his father had not yet died. The Lord Jesus does not ask us to turn away from our responsibilities to family or work, but He does ask that we put Him first. Perhaps we really wish to serve Him, but we feel that there are too many other responsibilities to allow us to do so. We do not enter His service to run away from responsibilities, but when we have entered it He will ensure that we can fulfil our responsibilities. This man did have concerns about important issues, but in following the Lord Jesus, he could leave these issues with Him.

The devil will tell you that the Christian lives a wasted life; the Lord tells you that it is the only fully satisfying life. Is this the life which you desire? By obedience to the Scriptures, by prayer, by holiness of life this can be yours, for God's great desire is to bless us. The issue is not whether God will give, but whether we are prepared to lay aside every weight and the sin which drags us down (Heb 12.1), to devote all our energy to serving Him, and to find, as a result, in this life and in eternity, rewards which are above all that we can ask or think.

CHAPTER 2

What about Baptism?

Now you are saved, but have you been baptised? This question would have seemed strange to a believer from the early church because each convert was baptised as soon as possible after salvation. The longest recorded period of time between conversion and baptism was three days, in the case of Saul of Tarsus (Acts 9). You would agree that, taking the circumstances into account, he was baptised as soon as it was possible. If you have not been baptised we ask that you consider the questions: "Is it necessary?", and, "Would my spiritual life suffer if I ignored baptism?".

Before answering these questions we must deal with misunderstandings that we find from time to time. Some think themselves to be too immature or without sufficient knowledge of the Scriptures to be baptised. They feel that they must study the Bible in greater depth before baptism is considered. In response to this it has to be said that there is no standard of maturity or knowledge of Scripture to which we must attain before baptism. When Philip the evangelist preached in the city of Samaria it is recorded that when the people "believed Philip...they were baptized, both men and women" (Acts 8.12). Following this, Philip was in Gaza when the Ethiopian eunuch was saved, and he was immediately baptised (Acts 8.26-40). Lydia, a seller of purple cloth from the city of Thyatira, heard the gospel, and it is recorded of her, "whose heart the Lord opened", as a result of which she was baptised (Acts 16.14-15). The jailor in Philippi was also baptised immediately after salvation, as was his house, which no doubt included his family and those of his household, who had also believed (Acts 16.33). Crispus, the chief ruler of the synagogue in Corinth, together with many other Corinthians heard and believed and they, too, were baptised (Acts 18.8). It is clear that none of those who were baptised waited until they had been further taught in spiritual things. They did not wait until they were more mature in the faith. They believed and were baptised as an act of obedience.

What is clear from these examples is that baptism followed salvation. There is no record in the Word of God of infants being baptised or sprinkled. Baptism is not the declaration of parents that they will bring up their children in a Christian environment, nor that the child has by that act become part of the "church". Those who were "sprinkled" as babies, as was the writer, must still be baptised after salvation, as the act carried out when they were young has no validity before God.

Others may feel that baptism is a milestone in spiritual life, after which they will be expected to live according to higher spiritual standards, as if there were two standards acceptable to God, one for before baptism and one for after. The truth is that when we are saved our lives are changed, and as babes in Christ, we start a lifetime of developing maturity in the things of Christ. Nevertheless, young believers have stated that they feel free to engage in pastimes which they would require to drop if they were baptised, and, as they are, they have greater freedom to enjoy their youth.

All this shows a basic misunderstanding of salvation. Baptism is not a second spiritual new start. It is a public acknowledgement of a change that has already taken place. If you are saved, the features of the new life should be shown now. There is no interlude after salvation during which you need not submit to the claims of the Lordship of Christ.

But, some will argue, the Bible does not teach us that baptism is necessary for salvation to be ours, so why then should I be baptised, and in what way would I suffer should I refuse? Baptism is the first test of our obedience. It was an essential part of the commission given to the disciples by the Lord Jesus

- to go, make disciples, and baptise them (Mt 28.19). To refuse baptism is to refuse the command of Christ, and, if we profess to be saved, we must realise how serious disobedience is. No matter what claim He makes on us we should obey, whether we understand the full significance of the act or not. Right at the beginning of our Christian life we are faced with a decision that tests the reality of our profession that He is our Lord. To obey Him is to acknowledge His Lordship; to disobey is to deny it. The secret of a developing Christian life is obedience, and if we fail at the first test it will compromise all our future attempts to serve Him. It will be an outstanding issue, constantly on our conscience, which must be resolved before further progress can be made.

Baptism is, second, a public acknowledgement of an invisible transaction; it is a test of our determination to witness. When you were saved no one could see what had taken place. You experienced the change, but it was not visible at that point to others. Baptism is your opportunity to declare to others what has happened. The question is whether you are prepared to witness publicly for the Lord Jesus. If this initial act of witness is not carried out, how can you hope to be effective in testifying to others of the power of the gospel? Public witnessing at work and in other places can, at times, be difficult. Young believers may feel embarrassed when faced with the hostility or even the laughter of those to whom they have been testifying. Your baptism is a good, a Scriptural, foundation on which to build a life of testimony. You will learn that the more often you speak of Christ the smaller the obstacles seem to be.

The third fact to note is that baptism is an act of identification with Christ, and we must not lose sight of its doctrinal significance. By this means we symbolise our death, burial, and resurrection with the Lord Jesus Christ, thus acknowledging the effect on our lives of His work on the cross. It is by considering this aspect of baptism that we see the importance of being baptised in the Scriptural manner of total immersion in water after confession of faith in Christ as Lord and Saviour. The Bible does not teach the baptism of infants by sprinkling (or any other means), for they are unable to make a decision to accept Christ, or the baptism of unbelievers, for they have not been buried with Christ to rise and walk in newness of life.

In Romans 6 Paul introduces baptism when dealing with the question, "Shall we continue in sin?" - shall we continue to live as we did before salvation? It has long been argued by some that to believe in the Lord Jesus as Saviour is not incompatible with a life which continues to go on in the old style that characterised pre-salvation days. This cannot be so, because when we were saved we died to sin. The meaning of this is that we passed out of the sphere where sin held sway. Burial is the ultimate public acknowledgment that a death has taken place, and when we are buried with Christ by baptism into death we are acknowledging that we have died to the old life and are finished with the world. Please note that when you are baptised you are not stating that the change which salvation brings will be seen from that moment on, you are stating that a change has already taken place when you accepted the Saviour. In this new life we are no longer the slaves of sin, as death annuls all obligations and ends all servitude to sin.

The challenge is therefore issued to you from the Word of God. As the Ethiopian eunuch, to whom reference has already been made, realised immediately after he had accepted the truth of the gospel, there is nothing to hinder your baptism. If it has not taken place, *you* are the hindrance. It is now time to put the matter right by bowing in obedience to the Lord who died for you and publicly declaring your allegiance to Him by following Him through the waters of baptism.

CHAPTER 3

What about Assembly Fellowship?

Following salvation and baptism the question facing a young believer is, "Should I seek assembly fellowship?". The God who in creation "setteth the solitary in families" (Ps 68.6) has the same desire for His spiritual children, and the Acts of the Apostles, with the teaching of the epistles, shows us that believers did gather together and work together. They were not loners going their own way and living and working independently of each other.

It was the practice of these early believers to meet together as a local church. This gathering, or "assembly", was the means through which the Christians enjoyed fellowship and served God.

With which local church then should we seek fellowship? A local church consists of those who are saved, baptised, and gather together to break bread on the first day of the week, to pray, to teach the Scriptures, and to preach the gospel. A fuller description of a local assembly is not possible in this short chapter. When we come to consider fellowship, we should seek to join ourselves to the assembly which is local to us. In a village or small town this can usually be easily identified, as there will be one, or possibly two, assemblies in the town.

In a city, however, what is "local"' to us may, in some situations, be more difficult to identify. Where you live equidistant from two or more assemblies let the size of the assembly weigh heavily in your choice - that which is smaller needs your help most. When we live in an area where a number of assemblies exist, there is always the temptation to pass a small assembly and to attend one that is larger, and to justify this by stating, for example, that we need the company of young people, or that the small assembly is "dull", or "not active enough". Please do not think in this way. If it is company you desire you can enjoy fellowship at conferences, Saturday night meetings, etc. Remember your presence is strengthening your local assembly and may lead to others seeking fellowship with you. If the assembly does not seem active enough you can change this; small assemblies are pleased to receive help in the work of the gospel. Large centralised assemblies, drawing their numbers from a wide area where other small assembles exist, is not the New Testament pattern.

Is it important that you seek assembly fellowship? It is necessary, because we are warned not to forsake "the assembling of ourselves together" (Heb 10.25). This neglect may be caused by a wish to avoid the responsibilities which fellowship brings, or by the apparent attractiveness of interests which we know are incompatible with fellowship in a local church. Let us remember that to forsake is to desert or abandon, and we will be called to account at the Judgment Seat of Christ for such failure. If matters such as these are keeping you back, consider seriously the issues and remember that no earthly attraction or the desire for the easy life is worth placing before eternal reward.

It is vital because we need the local church! There we will find those who have been gifted to teach and edify the believers, and we need the benefit which can be gained from this. Personal Bible study must not be neglected, but this can be helped greatly by our being taught by those who are able to expound Scripture. Within a local church, as in all families, many different personalities are to be found. Through this we learn to live together in peace and to develop the Christian graces of patience, understanding, and love towards each other, a most important teaching process in the development of Christ-1ikeness.

It is essential because the local church needs us! All believers have received spiritual gifts for use in the service of the Lord

Jesus. The gifts that we have received will be of benefit to others, and if we do not join in the fellowship of the local believers we are denying them what Christ has given. Has He made a mistake? Is our gift unnecessary? Surely not!

It is crucial because the Lord Jesus Christ is there! "Where two or three are gathered together in my name, there am I in the midst of them" (Mt 18.20). Whenever the believers gather together the Lord is present, and where He is, we wish to be. This is a privilege and an honour which none who understand its greatness would willingly neglect. We have professed that He is Lord, and one way in which we can show this openly is by attending the gatherings which He honours and ennobles with His presence.

Is it important that I am active? Yes, of great importance! "Can I not," you may say, "enjoy the fellowship of a local church, but simply move along as a passenger with little participation in the work carried on?" Such a question betrays a lack of understanding of fellowship. Attending the Breaking of Bread or being a "Sunday-only Christian" is not being in fellowship in a local church. Saints may be forced reluctantly by age or by ill health into this situation, and the Lord will give credit for desires to gather which cannot be fulfilled, but where lack of interest and feeble excuses are the order of the day there is something sadly amiss.

In 1 Corinthians 12.14-26 Paul likens the local church to a human body. He shows that each member of the body is essential to the effective working of the whole; the ear, the hand, the eye, the foot, all have their role to play. The foot does not, because of its lower position in the body, grumble against the hand, and the eye does not, because of its higher position, look with disdain on the hand. If the hand does not function the whole body is denied its abilities. Similarly, if I do not function the whole local church suffers. I should not look with envy on those who have what appears to be a more prominent gift, nor with disdain on those who seem to be gifted in a more lowly way. If I deliberately do not use one of my arms it will gradually lose the power to function. Likewise if I fail to use the gifts which I have been given they will still be present, but not with the power to be used effectively. All members of the body are necessary and are interdependent.

It is important because of the Judgment Seat! At the Judgment Seat of Christ my work in the local church will be reviewed, and if it is "gold, silver, (or) precious stones" I will receive a reward. Otherwise I will suffer loss (1 Cor 3.11-15). It is not only important to be active in the assembly, but it is necessary to be active in a Scriptural way and, equally important, to do what we can with a spiritual attitude. Is such a reward not worth living and working for? Is this not a spiritual ambition worth striving after? Do not let laziness, other interests, personality clashes, or any other encumbrance keep you back from going in for the very best, building up the saints, serving Christ, spreading the gospel in and through your local assembly.

CHAPTER 4

What about my Spiritual Gift?

As you look at the work which requires to be done in your local assembly you will be faced with the question, "What spiritual work am I fitted to do?". How, then, do you determine this and develop the gift you have?

Let us begin by reminding ourselves that the days in which we live are days of a spiritual message. That is, the gospel is a spiritual gospel; believers offer up spiritual sacrifices, and constitute a spiritual house. In order to enable this spiritual work to be carried out there has been given to the Church spiritual gifts, and it is important to learn that a spiritual work can only be carried out by spiritual means. Spiritual gifts are, therefore, God-given endowments for the carrying out of His work through the saints.

When considering what your contribution might be, you must recognise that there is a difference between natural abilities and spiritual gifts. Although you may be a good public speaker, this does not indicate that you are gifted as an evangelist or a teacher (nor does it indicate that you are not). Although you may be a good administrator and get on well with people, this does not mean that you are a shepherd of the flock. You will find lists of spiritual gifts in Romans 12.6-8, 1 Corinthians 12.8-10, and Ephesians 4.11. Some of these gifts are with us today and some are not. Our present purpose is not to discuss this aspect of the question: sufficient to state that apostles, prophets, and the sign gifts of tongues etc. are not with us today. As you look down these lists, what gift or gifts do you consider you have been given?

There are some that may look more attractive than others - would it not be much better to be an evangelist or a teacher than to be a help? Or is exhorting not much more attractive than serving (the word "ministry" means to serve, although today we use it mainly when referring to the service of teaching)?

Start, therefore, by endeavouring to establish what gift or gifts you have. It is good practice to make this a matter of prayer. In that way you can honestly face the issue of, "What am I fitted to do?". Through prayerful consideration you may find that desires will be born in your heart to engage in a particular line of service, or opportunities, or even completely unexpected circumstances, may be presented to you which serve to reveal the gift that you have been given. Remember that it is not the way of God to give a gift and then to place a maze in front of you through which you must find a path in order to identify your gift. In this, as in everything in spiritual life, if you seek you will find. All believers have spiritual gift, and it is your responsibility to settle where you can be of service.

A good pointer is to work in the local assembly and you will discover that it soon becomes clear what you are fitted to do. You will find that there are tasks which you feel you can carry out effectively and there are others which do not fit so readily. If you do not "pull your weight" in the local assembly your gifts will not be recognised or developed.

As a second pointer, it is good to keep in mind that you are not always the best judge of what is your gift. It can be that you have a thirst to exercise a gift which you do not have. The opinion of your brethren is a good indication of whether you are engaged in the correct line of service. If you consider yourself to be a gospel preacher but you are never asked to preach the gospel, give this fact consideration and do not just blame your brethren for being short-sighted or jealous. If you consider yourself to be a help when saints are in great difficulty but the assembly seems to keep you away from those going through such times, think on the significance of this. To pursue a gift which you do not have can lead to bitterness and frustration, as well as leaving to others the work for which you *are* fitted.

A third helpful indicator is the response of those who receive the benefit of the use of your gift. If you seek to be a "help" in difficult circumstances, do those in difficulty find they are helped by your efforts? If you teach, are the saints edified? If the results of your work are never beneficial you must examine the course you are taking. I am not suggesting that you should look for praise from others, or that everyone will always approve of how you exercise gift, but the pointers mentioned above, if followed, would preserve you from much anguish through seeking to carry out a work that God has not given you to do.

Remember, too, it is possible to have spiritual gift and neglect it. Paul exhorts Timothy to "Neglect not the gift that is in thee" (1 Tim 4.14). Neglect comes through not recognising the value of the gift, and is an indication of a lack of interest in, and a failure to appreciate the value of, spiritual things. If you value what God has given, you will want to develop it so that it can be used in the service of the Master, making you "a workman that needeth not to be ashamed" (2 Tim 2.15). How then is this done?

The first thing to develop is Christian character which will reflect well on your work. Timothy is again exhorted in this way: "Take heed unto thyself' (1 Tim 4.16). You cannot preach the gospel to others if your life is not lived according to the gospel. There is no point in telling others to "turn to God from idols" if your life is filled with modern "idols". There will be little response to teaching separation from the world if you are enmeshed in it. There will be few benefits in seeking to be helpful if your manner is ungracious. In the world men say, "If one is capable it matters little how one lives", but that is not true of spiritual service. Reading the Scriptures, engaging in prayer, attendance at the assembly gatherings, are all essential if you want to make your progress apparent to all.

Having read the conclusions reached in chapter 3, you will now understand that in order for your gift to be developed it must be used. "Stir up the gift of God, which is in thee" (2 Tim 1.6) is further valuable advice. Do not neglect your gift or it will never be as effective as God intended. If you have the gift of an evangelist and never speak to others about the gospel you will never learn how to handle the objections which they raise nor the problems which they have. Keep at it and see your usefulness grow.

Read carefully 1 Corinthians 13 and learn that the motive in the use of gift must always be love. You do not work to prove yourself more gifted than others; you do not serve to score points off others. Show the features of this chapter and your service will be enhanced beyond measure.

One final word of warning! Whatever gift you have you must show no pride in it. Nor should you feel a spiritual inferiority complex if you do not have the gift you wish. God makes no mistakes. So give yourself wholly to these things. You have a work to do and have been fitted by God to do it. Do not let worldliness, idleness, or lack of interest deny you this privilege.

CHAPTER 5

What about Studying the Scriptures?

Having come into the fellowship of a local church, a young believer who has a desire to serve God must be given over to the study of the Scriptures. In the present day it is obvious that less time is spent in this pursuit than by previous generations. We have a wide range of activities open to us in our leisure hours, the diversity and attractiveness of which have lured many away from the profitable, necessary, and time-consuming task of applying themselves to the systematic study of the Word of God. Any who do pursue this study find it far from being dry and irrelevant. It becomes absorbing, interesting, and of great spiritual benefit. The question to all is: Are you prepared to devote yourself in this way, spend the time which is necessary, and realise the blessings which it brings?

As we address ourselves to the study of the Scriptures some lessons must be constantly kept before us. There is the danger of studying simply to acquire knowledge or to prepare for public preaching. If this is our only motive we will fail in the most important issue, that of hearing the voice of the Holy Spirit speaking to us. Remember also that the Bible is so vast that no one person can assimilate all its truth. Given our limited powers of understanding and the relatively short number of years at our disposal, we do need the help and teaching of others to fill out our knowledge of the Word of God. No one has a monopoly of understanding.

Why then should we study the Word of God? The Scriptures give many answers to this question, but these are summed up in 2 Timothy 3.16-17: "All Scripture is given by inspiration of

God, and is profitable for doctrine, for reproof, for correction, for instruction in righteousness: that the man of God may be perfect, throughly furnished unto all good works". Scripture is God-breathed, that is, it owes its origin and content to the Holy Spirit. In this Book God speaks and who would not be interested in knowing more of this? As we handle Scripture we are dealing with the very words of God, and, confident of its infallibility, we learn of the past, the present, and the future. There is unfolded to us the great purpose of God which makes the student of Scripture more intelligent than any politician as to the forces at work in our world.

Note also that Scripture is profitable. There is blessing to be had from the Word of God. So many books are of dubious benefit and can easily affect the thinking and damage the testimony of the reader. This Book, however, is completely different, as the study of it can only profit. Scripture teaches us doctrine. God sets no premium on ignorance, and, through the Scriptures, imparts knowledge to us. We do well to seek to learn of the doctrine, for in every area of life ignorance is unhelpful in equipping us for a task, and spiritual life is no exception to this. Do not be misled by those who say that experience is greater than doctrine. The most useful servants are those who are taught, thus having an understanding of what the Master expects of us.

We study Scripture also because it reproves us. As we read it we find that our consciences are searched and we are convicted and warned of what is erroneous in our lives. Following reproof we are instructed how to correct our lives. How practical this all is. The study of the Scriptures shows us the things in our lives which we must change in order to make us of greater value in the service of the Master.

In addition to these benefits we will find that Scripture instructs us in righteousness. We are trained and disciplined in righteousness, which will keep us in an upright state before God. Thus the reproof and the correction take effect and things are set right.

We can see, then, that Bible study is not merely gaining a

mental knowledge of the contents of the Bible. If carried out with true motives it will have a profound practical effect on the way we live our lives. The purpose of it all is that "the man of God may be perfect" that is, attain maturity, "throughly furnished unto all good works". We are to be fully equipped and put in readiness for the work of serving God. With a knowledge of the Scriptures we will be prepared for whatever circumstances we meet, whether it is the need to comfort, to teach, to reprove, to speak of the Lord Jesus, or simply to enjoy conversing with others who have an interest in the Word of God.

Scripture study is therefore vital in our training for the service of the Master. With it we come to know how our lives can be pleasing to God and how our assemblies can function for His glory. Without it we will be spiritual "lightweights" tossed about with every new fashion and theory and with a very cloudy view of how God's work should be carried on.

But, you may ask, when should we study? You will find that your ability to take in what you are reading will diminish as the years pass; it is vital, therefore, to study when you are young. Study must be carried out on a daily basis. If it is haphazard and irregular there will be no continuity and the benefits will be reduced. Decide which part of the day is best for you. Some can study in the morning before leaving for work, finding the peace and quiet invaluable. Others find that evening is more suitable and can work on long into the small hours when others have retired for the night. Above all, you must discipline yourself to continue in your chosen programme. Do not regard it as an extra which can be put aside when it is not too convenient, but give it the high priority which it demands. For those who are married it is worth remembering the invaluable part which a wife plays in this. A good husband will not use Bible study as an excuse to leave all household tasks to his wife, but a good wife will recognise that her husband does need time to be alone with the Bible. Nor should we forget that wives also need time to read the Scriptures and meditate on what God is saying. Are we studying the Scriptures or is our reading simply a few hurried verses each day? Start now and find how challenging and absorbing your studies will become!

The next question which arises is: How should we study? The Word of God is a library of sixty-six books, written by many authors under the inspiration of the Holy Spirit, over a period of about 1,600 years. The first question, therefore, we ask is: where do we start? From the beginning we must approach the Scriptures correctly. Learn the overall plan of the Bible, and how God has dealt with men in different ways at different times (you will come to know these times as dispensations). You will then see that, for instance, we do not find direct teaching about the Church in the Old Testament and that, despite modern hymnology, the Lord Jesus is not our King (He is King of Israel). If, as you read this, you feel that such things are details which appear to be "old-fashioned hair-splitting", you will progress little further in your study of this great Book. Reading a few verses haphazardly is completely unsatisfactory and will lead to disillusionment and the feeling that this is an uninteresting Book with no coherent plan. Study must be systematic, so select one book to which you will direct your attention and read this over a number of times until you become familiar with its structure. At first select one of the smaller books of the Bible. To help you, in addition to the Authorised (King James) Version, read the Revised Version and the New Translation of J. N. Darby (good suggestions to those who ask what you would like for a birthday present). By comparing these versions you will heighten your understanding of the text. At this stage answer a number of questions.

1. Who wrote the book?
2. Why was it written?
3. When was it written?
4. How is the book structured?
5. How does it relate to others books in the Bible?

Now look at the book in greater detail! Study each section and then each verse within the section. The level of detail to which you take this will depend on the nature of the book which you are studying and on your own determination to squeeze as much as is possible from the text, but do remember that diligent detailed study is well rewarded. Remember that Old Testament books are of great value, and do not neglect them. There are a plentiful supply of helps available to the student. A suggested "first buy" list (or a top up for the birthday/ Christmas present suggestion box) is:

1. Strong's *Concordance*
2. *Expository Dictionary of Bible Words*, by W.E.Vine
3. *Theological Wordbook of the Old Testament*, by Harris/ Archer/Waltke (Eds).

These will be of great assistance in coming to an accurate understanding of the detailed text. Our English translations sometimes, for instance, translate the same Greek word by the use of two or more different English words. The opposite is also true, in that different Greek words can be translated by the use of the same English word. Use of these tools will let you see exactly what is written without the necessity of becoming a self-taught Greek "expert". Obtain books by reliable teachers who can provide further insight into Scripture. Young believers still can receive much benefit from C. H. Macintosh on the Pentateuch, Moule on Paul's Epistles etc. Gradually you will build a library and be able to discern those whose works are of benefit, and those who are unreliable. Many of the books you will not read from cover to cover, but you will scan them, and use them as reference volumes in your studies.

Acquire the habit of taking notes. It is true to say that there are probably as many note-taking systems as there are students of the Scriptures, but a few basic pointers will be helpful. Open a note book or file for each book in the Bible. Into this enter outlines of the book and more detailed notes on the text. If you wish to do this in great detail, in for instance the epistles, have a page for each verse, write at the top of the page the translations from the versions which you may use and any notes you wish to retain. From time to time you will add to these and build a valuable reference file. The use of a wide-margin or loose-leave Bible can also be helpful in noting the meanings of words, outlines of the book etc. Ensure, however, that you use the pen recommended by the publishers - anything else will disfigure the pages.

Never forget that Bible study is not done in isolation. How much better will be the results if you attend meetings where the Word is taught, and if you discuss Scripture with older brethren able to teach. Raise any problems you have, ask if conclusions you have reached are correct. Read, meditate, listen, and ask!

A letter written over 800 years ago gave advice which is still valuable. "Moreover, you must get leisure for definite reading at a definite hour. Reading left to chance, and reading passages at haphazard, does not edify, but renders the mind unstable, and what is lightly lodged there, lightly withdraws. But it must be dwelt upon with faculties concentrated; and the mind needs to become accustomed to the study. For the Scriptures require to be read in the same spirit in which they were written, and can only so be understood. You will never enter into the sense of Paul until by the exercise of good intention in reading him and by assiduous meditation you have imbibed his spirit. You will never understand David till by actual experience the feelings of his psalms have become yours. And so with the rest. And in every Scripture study is as different from mere reading as friendship is from entertaining a guest, and social affection from accidental salutation...If in reading the writer seeks God, everything that he reads co-operates with him to this end, and it captivates his feeling and brings his whole sense of the passage into the obedience of Christ. If, on the other hand, the feeling of the reader declines upon some other end, it drags everything with it, and he finds nothing so holy or pious in Scripture as either by vain glory or a distorted feeling or a corrupt understanding that may not minister to his harm or vanity".

Determine now to give yourself to this noble and profitable task. Study carefully, prayerfully, and with a reverence for God.

Study for your own benefit and put into practice the lessons learned. By doing so you will ensure that you are a well-equipped servant of the Master.

CHAPTER 6

What about my Prayer Life?

In Luke 11, as the disciples observed the Lord Jesus engaging in prayer, there was born into the heart of one of them the thought that his own prayer life fell far short of what it should be. Immediately the Saviour ceased, the request leapt to his lips, "Lord, teach us to pray" (v.1), a desire that will be in the hearts of all who really want to be followers of the Master.

The problem of prayer can be one of the greatest challenges faced by young believers. Many who seek to engage in private prayer expect to see instant answers to their requests and to have a warm feeling that God has heard. When this does not take place they can become disappointed and lose interest in prayer, which soon becomes a mechanical task with little thought or effort being expended. What a loss when this takes place!

These expectations are due to a lack of understanding of what prayer is and of how God acts. The necessity, and the value of prayer are seen in the life of the Lord Jesus. In Luke 6.12 we see Him continuing all night in prayer before He chose the twelve. As He faced a great decision He retired to pray to God. In Matthew 14.23 He retired to pray after a great day of blessing. In Mark 1.35 He went out a great while before day to pray, taking time before a day of activity when all men were seeking Him. Thus we see how vital prayer was to Him and how every day found Him so engaged before God. All service was the subject of prayer, and after the task was complete He prayed again, thankful to His God.

How then ought we to pray? Note from the references above

that the Lord Jesus set aside specific times to pray. This can be a difficult discipline to sustain. In the mornings we have so little time, in the evenings we are so busy and so tired, and during the day there is no suitable opportunity. Do not, however, let these thoughts hold you back. Set aside a time every day, ensuring that you are not seeking to achieve the impossible. Better a slightly shorter time that you achieve than a long prayer session which it is impossible to maintain. When you pray you will find sometimes that your mind wanders or that sleep can overwhelm you. To avoid this consider before you pray the matters before you. You can even engage in a series of shorter prayers with a few moments between each for meditation and consideration of the subjects which you are about to raise in the presence of God. Above all, prepare before prayer! It is said of A. T. Pierson that he kept a prayer diary, entering on one page the matters which were the object of his prayers, and on the opposite page the answer which God gave, no matter how long he had to wait for it.

But why, you may ask, should we pray? Things seem to go along whether we are a praying people or not, so why bother? Note, first, that we have already seen that a Christ-like life must be a prayerful life. If He found it necessary to be a Man of Prayer, it should be an essential part of our lives. Prayer is a confession of our dependence on God. A day without prayer is a day when we say that we do not need Him.

Prayer is an opportunity to show in His presence that His will is our will. When, for example, we pray for the salvation of sinners we are praying according to His will, and how delightful this is to Him. As we go to pray, what then should be on our hearts and in our prayers?

Always remember that prayer is thankful. Good practice is always to start by expressing our thankfulness for all He has done. For saving us, for preserving us, for opportunities to serve, for the lessons we have been taught, even for the things which we would rather He had not taken us through, "...be ye thankful" (Col 3.15). Do not, however, confine your thanks to what has been done for you, but consider what He has done for others and follow the example of the apostle Paul by including these in your prayers.

Learn through prayer that prayer is powerful. In the difficulties of life it is good to know that we have resources which the world knows nothing of. In Philippians 4.6 we learn that prayer is the answer to anxiety, which is replaced with the peace of God. We may not know all the answers but we are promised peace in the midst of the vicissitudes of life. Remember, however, no prayer - no peace! In the work of evangelism, and in establishing the saints, prayer is a vital ingredient. Look at the prayer life of Paul and see how he desired the prayers of the saints for the work to which he put his hand.

If you engage in prayer you will learn that prayer is helpful. In 2 Corinthians 1 Paul speaks of the Corinthians "helping together by prayer" (v.11). Their prayers had been of help to Paul in the difficulties through which he had passed. Believers do often need help of a practical nature when they are beset with problems, but remember that practical help should be in addition to the greatest help of all, our remembrance of them in prayer. They will experience help being given; this is not an abstract theory, it works!

After prayer we sometimes feel no different, so has it been of any value? Elijah was a man with feelings like ours, and he prayed and God heard, but Scripture does not tell us that he "felt good" or experienced "excitement". No, the way to ensure that our prayers are heard is found in Hebrews 5.7. The prayers of the Lord Jesus were heard in that He feared. Because His life was lived in the fear of God, with a reverence for Him and a desire to please Him, the prayers were heard. This then is the lesson for us: a godly life gives the assurance that He hears every prayer.

How easy, however, it is to give up. No one but God sees us in private prayer and, when we feel discouraged, it can be one of the first things to go. But Paul exhorts us to "Continue in prayer" (Col 4.2), to persist in prayer. If you show that persistence you will be able to look back and see when God answered your prayers. Wonder will fill your heart that the God and Father of our Lord Jesus Christ heard you, and graciously answered your prayers. That experience, with no false excitement or public acclamation, is one which you will never forget and which will confirm your faith as you continue in His service.

CHAPTER 7

What about God's Will for me?

The delight of any believer is to do the will of God. The difficulty is discerning what the will of God for us is. The first question which was asked by Paul after conversion was, "Who art thou, Lord?", and the second was, "What wilt thou have me to do?" (Acts 9.5-6). Thus Paul's first desire after salvation was to carry out the will of God. Many years later, having put this desire into practice, and having endured the joys and difficulties associated with that desire, Paul describes in Romans 12.2 three vital features of the will of God.

First, the will of God is good, in the sense of being beneficial. There are benefits in carrying out His will. It is not merely adherence to some code of conduct which we find restrictive. It has a beneficial effect on our lives. Second, the will of God is acceptable, in the sense of being well-pleasing. Thus God is well-pleased with the life of one who is doing His will. Third, the will of God is perfect, in the sense that it needs nothing added to it.

We have only one life, and it would be tragic to spend it endeavouring to do what He never intended us do, or even spending our years making no attempt to discern the will of God. Some of us may find that despite seeking to know the will of God we are constantly in a mood of doubt as to whether we are carrying this out. We listen to others who seem to be so sure that what they are doing is of God, and we wonder what prevents us having the same convictions.

We should be in no doubt that this is an issue of great consequence. From Colossians 1.9 we learn that Paul's prayer for the Colossians was that they "might be filled with the knowledge of his will in all wisdom and spiritual understanding". It is on the basis of this that they will be able to "walk worthy of the Lord unto all pleasing, being fruitful in every good work, and increasing in the knowledge of God". Walking worthy of Him is therefore dependent on knowing His will.

The first thing we must learn is that there are certain conditions that must be fulfilled in order to learn the will of God. Romans 12.1 gives us the first of these. We are to present our bodies a living sacrifice, holy, acceptable unto God which is our reasonable service. This implies a determined devotion to be consecrated wholly to God. There is little point in seeking His will if we are not prepared to be obedient to Him. To be as consecrated as this involves turning away from the world and refusing to order our lives by worldly standards. Thus, we are not conformed to this age. Again, it is not possible to seek God's will if we live according to the principles and standards of the world. The two simply will not mix.

When we present our bodies, and live a life not conforming to the world, we can prove, or put to the test, that good, and acceptable, and perfect will of God. Would each of us not want to see this in our own circumstances? The challenge is to put God to the test and see His will becoming a reality in our lives. First hand experience of God at work - what a prize for which to aim!

The same aim of proving what is acceptable to the Lord is found in Ephesians 5.10. In doing this Paul teaches that we must keep away from the works of darkness and redeem the time. The picture drawn is that of one who is determined to live a life in fellowship with God, and is exercised before Him as to how every day should be lived. Living like that, we can understand what the will of the Lord is for every day.

Having established these conditions, we now turn to certain specific things pointed out to us as being the will of God. In 1 Thessalonians 5.18 we learn that it is the will of God that we should be thankful. This spirit of thankfulness is not to be for the pleasant things of life alone, but for everything. In Ephesians 6.6 the servant is seen doing the will of God when he is working with honest sincerity, not only when his master is present, but at all times. Sacrificial giving is also seen in 2 Corinthians 8.5 as fulfilling His will. First, the Macedonians gave themselves and then they gave of their substance. Self-sacrifice comes before material sacrifice. Submission to the civil authorities, so that others may have nothing to accuse us of, is another feature of doing His will. So we see that thankfulness, sincerity at work, sacrifice, and submission are all characteristics which we strive to work out daily.

"But", you may ask, "that is fine as a general guide for conduct, but how do I know the will of God for specific situations which arise? These features which you have given us are those which we already try to achieve. How do I know the pathway to take when I am faced with alternatives?"

Paul was confronted with such a situation in Acts 16. The question with which he and his companions had to deal concerned the future direction of their service in the gospel. After travelling through Galatia they were forbidden by the Holy Ghost to go into Asia. They then turned and attempted to set out in the direction of Bithynia but the Spirit suffered them not. We do not know exactly how the Spirit let them know that they should not go in either of these directions, but circumstances may have made these journeys impossible. Following this, Paul had the vision of the man of Macedonia calling them over to help. Note that in v.10 it is Paul who sees the vision, but the whole party has to come to a decision. On what basis was this decision made? The key to this is the words used by Luke the writer. He was in that little group, and he tells us that they "assuredly gathered" that they should go into Macedonia. The force of the expression used is that they examined all the circumstances involved, they assessed them in relation to the other factors, they thought about them as a whole. When they brought all these things together, they determined the pathway down which they should travel.

What lessons can be drawn from this incident? We must allow that these men fulfilled the preconditions which we have already considered. Note, then, that this little group of gospel workers were not idling away the time. They were active in the service of God and were turning this way, seeking to travel that way, anxious to be carrying on with the task to which they had set their hand. God reveals His will to active believers, not to those who sit and wait, passing the time in a state of enthusiastic idleness.

It is significant, as has been noted above, that only Paul saw the vision, but that the whole party "assuredly gathered". We must take all the circumstances into account, weighing up all the issues involved, ensuring that nothing we plan is contrary to Scripture, and then prayerfully bring them all together and come to our conclusion. The decisions we reach must be the result of deep consideration before God, and He gives us all the indications required to reach a judgment which is according to His will. Opened doors, closed doors, personal responsibilities, need which we perceive has to be met, the gift which God has given us to use etc; all are involved in the decisions of life.

May our desire be to know the delight which David had in doing the will of God (Ps 40.8). This, for him, was not something to which he gave attention reluctantly. It was a joy to fulfil it. Should we then not seek to learn His will and know the joy of understanding the answer to the question asked by Paul, "What shall I do, Lord?" (Acts 22.10)?

CHAPTER 8

What about Worry?

To the casual observer the meal was going very well. The visitors seemed to be rested and content, and it would appear that the hostess could be happy with the hospitality which she had extended to the Lord Jesus. Such a thought was, however, far from her mind. The anxious hours of preparation, the stress of waiting for the arrival of her guests, and her constant vigilance as she organised the serving of the dishes, all had their effect. She was so overburdened that all enjoyment had gone out of the day. As she observed her sister sitting at the feet of the Saviour, Martha could contain herself no longer and cried out, "Lord, dost thou not care that my sister hath left me to serve alone?" (Lk 10.40). What then had changed the anticipated joy into frustration? We turn to the words of the Lord Jesus for the answer as He gently reminded her that it was care and trouble which had brought her to this state of anxiety. Worry had taken its toll.

Despite our attempts to know the will of God and put it into practice we find that into our lives there come from time to time circumstances which cause worry. This dark feeling hangs over us like a black cloud and, whatever we are doing, it is always there in the back of our minds, no matter how we seek to put it away. Day by day it is our constant companion, robbing us of all joy, and in extreme cases causing us physical pain and exhaustion. Issues arise in our lives which we would rather had never come in, and the worry and anxiety which they cause are with us constantly. However much we try to banish this feeling it still remains, and it seems to be impossible to get rid of it.

We wonder why it is that other Christians seem to worry less than we do, and, even when they are going through periods which would create in us great feelings of anxiety, they seem to be able to carry on without the signs of stress and concern which we would show in their situation. Our conclusion may be that they do not care as much as we do, or that they have a cold, indifferent attitude to the problems of life. We still ask ourselves, however, if that is really true. Another feature which we notice is that the worry meter in each of us is triggered at different points. Some people seem to worry constantly, and the level of their concern is as high when small things are occupying their minds, as it is when great issues have to be faced.

Worry can be the result of many differing causes. Family, work, health, assembly matters, and finance are some, but not all, of the factors. In some cases there are actions of our own which we bitterly regret, and in others there are reasons which are not of our own making. What then is worry? If we analyse our feelings carefully, we find that worry is that reaction which is caused by situations arising now, or which we feel may arise in the future, which are not as we would have them be. The effects of worry can be devastating. As it grows we find ourselves being weakened physically, our minds lose their sharpness, and our ability to work is diminished.

The Word of God teaches us how to handle such conditions. It does not tell us that we should simply be unconcerned about worrying issues, for that would be failing to fulfil our responsibilities. What we are taught is that there is a firm and understandable basis on which to act when worries oppress us. This is not merely an emotional knee-jerk reaction, but a course of action which can be substantiated from Scripture and by consideration of the issues involved. We are told not only what to do, but why we can have confidence in so acting.

The first thing we must observe is that the Bible does not teach us that the believer will be without care. Believers live in the same world as others and are subject to the same pressures and difficulties throughout life. Illness still comes, financial pressures still surround us, families still give cause for concern.

The difference between the Christian and others, however, is that believers are told in Scripture how to handle the cares and worries of life. Paul gives us excellent advice when he writes, "Be careful for nothing; but in everything by prayer and supplication with thanksgiving let your requests be made known unto God" (Phil 4.6). Thus, in answer to the question, "How do I tackle worry?", the Scriptures tell us to pray. As we have already observed, we are not told to go through life ignoring the problems which beset us. Nor is Paul suggesting a callous approach to the plight of others. He is rather giving us the prime lesson in handling care and worry - take it to the Lord in prayer. When we feel that anxiety of which he speaks, that which seems to be pulling us apart, to be drawing us in two directions, then let us bring our specific requests to God in prayer.

The promise which is given here is not that the problems will disappear, but that we will experience the peace of God in the midst of them. This peace is not due to our abdicating our responsibilities, but because of the confidence that we have that He is now with us in the circumstances. In answering our supplications God is pleased to keep both our hearts and minds through Christ Jesus: that is, our emotions and our intellect are guarded so that we are taken through the storm. This emphasises to us once again the supreme importance of prayer. If we do not pray we cannot expect to enjoy this peace, and will remain filled with concern, seeking to handle life's difficulties in our own strength.

Now that we have learned how to tackle the worries of life, we ask another question. How many of our cares can we bring to Him at the one time? Peter answers this: "Casting all your care upon him; for he careth for you" (1 Pet 5.7). There is no situation which is beyond Him, and we are exhorted to bring all our cares and cast them upon Him. Our shoulders may feel at times too weak, but we can turn to One who never will be overburdened. As a deliberate act therefore we have to take our cares and let Him bear the weight of them. This again is not an easy escape route, for they still are our cares, but it is an expression of our confidence in Him, based on the fact that He does have a genuine care for us. He seeks only our good and the care which He has for us will bring us through to where He wishes us to be. As we read the verses which surround this statement we will see that casting our care on Him is necessary if we would deal with the onslaught of the Adversary. A worried, burdened servant, seeking to carry all the weight himself, is too weakened to serve his Master profitably.

So many of the worries have to do with the problems of providing for the necessities of life. The Lord Jesus speaks of this in Matthew 6. In v.25 we have not to be anxious for the provision of these necessities, and in v.34 we have to have no anxiety about tomorrow. The basis for this is that we have around us the evidence of the care of God for His creatures, and, if He provides for fowls and clothes the grass of the field, He will do so for those who trust Him.

The Psalmist speaks from experience when he tells us to "Cast thy burden upon the Lord, and he shall sustain thee" (Ps 55.22). We note from this verse, as from Philippians 4, that there is an important condition for the enjoyment of the sustaining power of God in the midst of our troubles. Psalm 55 speaks of the righteous not being moved, and Philippians is filled with instruction as to how we must live for God. If we live as we like, with no attempt to please God, we cannot expect Him to carry our burdens, for in our manner of living we have declared that we do not need Him. Better far to live a righteous life, enjoying all that this brings, and, when worry intrudes, turning to Him in confidence and letting Him bear the load. Thus, as in all issues of life, obedience to the Scriptures will bring its reward.

CHAPTER 9

What about Worship?

What does the word "worship" convey to you? To many it brings to mind thoughts of stained glass windows and of great choirs singing or chanting. To you it may convey the impression of specific times which are set aside daily for worship, and of certain gatherings of the believers for the same purpose. Often we hear of the Breaking of Bread referred to as the "worship meeting", the implication being that this gathering is one in which worship is the dominant theme, whereas in others it is teaching believers or preaching to others which is the main purpose. Other "worship meetings" often consist of times of hymn singing or even of prayer and meditation. What, however, does the Bible tell us about worship?

The word worship means "to bow down and to kiss the ground". When this was done it was to acknowledge the presence of one who was great and worthy of homage. The first Hebrew mention of the word is in Genesis 18.2 when Abraham ran towards the three men who came to his tent and bowed himself to the ground. He was acknowledging the presence of One who was greater than himself and whom he addressed in v.3 as, "My Lord".

We also find the word in Genesis 22.5 and Abraham again is the speaker: "Abide ye here with the ass", he says to the young men who were accompanying him, "and I and the lad will go yonder and worship". On this occasion Abraham was travelling to the land of Moriah to offer up his son Isaac, and so we learn that worship involves obedience to God. Abraham was aware of the fact that in Moriah, on the mount, he would be entering the presence of God. The sacrifice of what was dear to him was worship, an acknowledgement of the greatness of the One who had commanded.

Very closely linked with worship is service. In Exodus 20.5 serving graven images is associated with bowing down, or worshipping them. Thus, what we worship we will serve. The Lord Jesus confirms this in Matthew 4.10 when He quotes Deuteronomy 6.13 to Satan in the wilderness: "Thou shalt worship the Lord thy God, and him only shalt thou serve".

We can now define worship as an acknowledgement of the greatness of God by being obedient to Him and thus serving Him. Worship is therefore an attitude towards God, and should be a constant state, not something which we turn off and on, nor something which is reserved for meetings of a special nature. It is the manner of those who are aware of the presence of God.

Under the Law, approach to God was limited to the Tabernacle and to the Temple. Only the Aaronic priest had this privilege. When Elkanah went to Shiloh it was to worship (1 Samuel 1.3), for there was the place where God had said His throne was to be found. To this place Israelites were required to come, bringing their sacrifices and acknowledging the greatness of the God who delivered them and kept them. Only as they obeyed the Scriptures which were committed to them were they able to worship, for without them they would be ignorant of the way of approach to the presence of God.

It should be noted that worship therefore can only be carried out if certain conditions are fulfilled. The willingly-disobedient believer cannot worship. When there are in our lives features which are not pleasing to Him this takes away from us the privilege of worship. In Psalm 29.2 we learn that worship must be carried out in the beauty of holiness. The Psalmist was referring to the holiness of the sanctuary where the Aaronic priesthood served God, but in so doing he teaches us the absolute necessity of holiness if we desire to enjoy the privilege of worship.

How then is worship expressed today? Remember that it is a

constant attitude to God and must be the basis of all our actions. Today we do not enjoy the presence of God only at an appointed place or at specific times. Paul tells the Philippians that they worship God in the spirit (the word "worship" here indicates doing temple service). Thus worship can be ours at all times and in all places.

We will, therefore, ask first of everything in which we are engaged, "Is this pleasing to God? Does it acknowledge His greatness by obeying Him?" Put that test against all to which you devote your mind, your time, and your energies.

We worship when we gather as believers to remember the Lord and to pray. Conscious of the presence of the Lord, our attitude is one of worship as we bring to Him our spiritual sacrifices for His acceptance. Have we really prepared our hearts for this and do we come with that which can be acceptably offered to Him?

We worship God when we give. Paul writes of the gift which he had received as "a sacrifice acceptable, well pleasing to God" (Phil 4.18). Sacrifice is something which has cost us. and not merely what we can spare and which is of no value to us whatsoever.

We worship when we preach the gospel. Paul writes of his gospel preaching as "ministering" (Rom 15.16) that is ministering as a priest in the gospel. He saw the Gentiles who were saved as an offering acceptable, sanctified by the Holy Ghost.

No area of our lives is excluded. In Romans 12.1 we are instructed to present our bodies as a living sacrifice. This is a priestly act and involves worship, just as with Abraham in Genesis 22. Note again that holiness is the condition and that such an act of worship is acceptable, or well-pleasing, to Him.

As already noted, each Lord's Day, as we gather to remember the Lord, we have a unique opportunity to engage all our faculties in worship. We are remembering the Lord unitedly as a local church and thanking God for Him. This should bring worship to the hearts of all believers present and thus cause us to pray, to sing together, and to thank God for His greatness and the gift which He gave when the Lord Jesus came to earth. Do we prepare for this? At this gathering we can express our worship in terms of thanksgiving for all He has done. Young brethren should be prepared to take part audibly and not always to be silent onlookers. Young sisters can contribute with their silent worship which is known to God and helps create that atmosphere of worship which is beyond price.

Let us also, however, observe from Scripture that it is possible to worship other gods and serve them. In Romans 1.25 we see men worshipping the creature rather than the Creator. Israel was constantly reminded of the dangers of worshipping the gods of the nations surrounding them. Ultimately Satan wishes us to put him in the place of God. He is quite prepared to put before us a substitute which he feels will tempt us away until our hearts are fully taken over and we find that our attitude to God is affected, and, indeed, other things (or people) take His place entirely.

The challenge to us in this is quite clear. Do we honour God in our lives, as we ought? Do we live an obedient life which is a prerequisite for worship? Do we ensure that what we do is acceptable to Him? That is worship and brings with it the joy of knowing His acceptance of our sacrifice.

CHAPTER 10

What about Evangelism?

It is doubtful if there ever has been an age when evangelism received so much attention amongst believers. Books are written, ministry is given, seminars are held, and countless discussions take place in order to identify the best way of spreading the gospel in our own localities. Yet despite this concentration of thought and effort it is rarely that we come upon a local assembly which is satisfied with its gospel outreach.

The other side of the picture is that many a young believer is in an assembly where there is little gospel activity apart from a weekly gospel meeting to which very few strangers ever come, and to which we would often be loathe to invite our neighbours and colleagues. This raises some very fundamental questions about evangelism and how we should tackle it today.

The initial thing to note is that the Lord Jesus did not first ask the disciples to come and be evangelists. There was something of prime importance necessary before that, something which seems to be little considered in all the teaching given and literature distributed on the subject nowadays. The invitation to the disciples was to come after Him and He would make them "to become fishers of men" (Mk 1.17). They were to concentrate on following Christ and He would make them what He wished them to be. We do not make ourselves evangelists. He makes us what we should be when we follow Him in obedience.

So, then, the prime qualification for serving Him is to be a follower. There is little value in telling others to come after the Saviour if we are not pursuing that pathway ourselves. At best that is naive and at worst it is dishonest. There is little point in telling lost souls that they must be obedient to John 3.16, but then turning to other sections of Scripture and excusing our disobedience by claiming that "they do not mean exactly what they say". Perhaps we may simply ignore sections which we know will affect our lives, or search until we find some so-called "explanation" which gives us an excuse to overlook the plain teaching of the Bible. Who gave us the right to use such double standards in handling the Word of God?

Another point to consider is that too often today we associate evangelism with large campaigns and immediate results. Such "campaigns" cannot, on their own, meet our responsibilities in the gospel, as, by their very nature, they take place at infrequent intervals. A regular assembly gospel campaign is an excellent part of gospel witness but what about the time in between?

Evangelism starts with our own personal testimony amongst those whom we meet and beside whom we work. The basic foundation of solid gospel work is a good testimony which commends the gospel and lets others see that our lives have something valuable and satisfying which is absent from the lives of others. Again there is little point in inviting people to come to a Saviour who can change their lives if our lives are little different from theirs.

In our presentation of the Saviour to others it is important not to fall into the trap of failing to give a true view of the gospel. In our anxiety to see a "decision" we sometimes minimise the change that will come over the life when salvation comes in. Be quite clear in explaining that He is Lord as well as Saviour, but be equally clear in stating that the power to be obedient to Him will be given when His Lordship is acknowledged.

Just as important is the error of trivialising the gospel, sometimes inadvertently. To become a Christian is a giant step, and whereas we do not put difficulties in the way of those who are enquiring, neither do we treat it lightly. A real sense of sin and God's hatred of it should never be omitted from the message of the evangelist.

What methods then should we use to pass on this message?

As with all areas of testimony it is wise to consult the Scriptures. The gospel is communicated by three kinds of sermon: the living sermon of a godly life, private conversation with an anxious soul, and public preaching in the hearing of unbelievers backed up by the distribution of literature. The first of these is alluded to by the Lord Jesus in Matthew 5.16: "Let your light so shine before men, that they may see your good works, and glorify your Father which is in heaven". An example of the second is to be found in Philip in Acts 8, where the importance of one anxious soul is emphasised by his being directed to go from fruitful gospel fields to the lonely desert at Gaza where he found one man reading the Scriptures and anxious to learn their truth. As far as the third is concerned there are countless examples in the Bible of the Word being preached fearlessly.

It is not given to everyone to preach publicly, but to those who do the question often before them is one of deciding where it should be done. The assembly gospel meeting is an excellent opportunity to bring strangers to hear the gospel. Let us ensure, however, that they are made to feel welcome. Remember that they will feel strange and unsure of the procedure. A good chairman can extend a welcome and explain what takes place without making it obvious that he is only speaking to one or two in the hall. Long drawn out gospel addresses using language which only believers understand is not evidence of a mature preacher, but rather of an unfit preacher. Gospel preaching must be clear, plain, and dignified, and yet fully present gospel truth. Gospel preaching is not to display the knowledge or gift of the preacher. If you are looking for examples to follow, examine the public teaching of the Lord and the sermons in the Acts.

But where else can we preach or testify? Open airs are still an excellent method, provided that they are held in places where you will be heard, for example in shopping centres or other such busy places. Do you have a local gala day? Why not use this as a place to distribute tracts and if possible preach. Do not expect people to respond the first time they hear the gospel. It is usually a series of incidents which form a chain and lead ultimately to conversion. What an honour to be a link in that chain!

We have often heard gospel work spoken of as a sales exercise - create the desire and then provide the product to meet that desire. How far short this falls. We do not create the desire, He does; we do not pressurise for a decision, the Holy Spirit convicts. Our part is to live before men a God honouring life and to preach the Word in season and out of season, leaving the results to Him.

CHAPTER 11

What about Giving?

As we study the Scriptures we will become aware of the fact that the subject of giving features prominently on the pages of the Word of God. Note, for example, that after reading through the heights of the teaching of 1 Corinthians 15 we are faced immediately with "the collection for the saints" (1 Cor 16.1), emphasising that this is part of "abounding in the work of the Lord". We will observe that in 2 Corinthians we find two chapters (chs.8-9) occupied with the subject, and further reading reveals many other references to the giving of the saints.

To live for the glory of God we must therefore face up to the demands of giving, and learn from Scripture how to use the resources which have been committed to our trust. Note, first, that giving is a sacrificial, priestly act. In Philippians 4.18 Paul writes of giving as "an odour of a sweet smell, a sacrifice acceptable, well pleasing to God". A sacrifice is something that is costly, involving the giving up of money or possessions which we could claim as our own and use in other ways. Let us learn, however, that all of value in the service of Christ involves sacrifice, and if we are not prepared for this we will never enter into the blessings given by the God who loves a cheerful giver (2 Cor 9.7). The priestly side of giving is seen in that the act is firstly for God's pleasure. What the Philippians gave not only met the needs of the apostle, but also was appreciated in heaven. How often we wonder what we can do that would be a joy to God. Here is something that can be done now!

What then does the Bible teach about how we should give?

Read the opening verses of 1 Corinthians 16 and you will see that three principles are laid out.

1. Giving must be systematic

The first day of the week is when we should determine how much we will give, and lay it aside for that purpose. The expression "lay by him in store" indicates the laying aside at home of the amounts determined. Our custom today is to bring the sum to the Breaking of Bread and place it in the bag or box, but you may also have laid a sum aside for a specific purpose which you keep until the appropriate time.

But, you may ask, in a day when many are paid on a monthly basis does this principle still stand? I submit that it does. By all means determine how much you should lay aside when your wages are received, but it is a good exercise to consider also this matter on the first day of each week, regarding it as much part of the responsibilities of the day as is the Breaking of Bread. Why is the first day of the week indicated? Surely it is the day when we remember the sacrificial giving of the Lord Jesus. He is the great incomparable example of sacrifice, and consideration of Him will move us to give.

2. Giving is expected of all

"Let every one of you", writes Paul, "lay by him in store". No exceptions are considered. You may think you have too little money to give, but no matter how small your contribution is it should be given. Remember the widow's mite and how much this was appreciated by the Lord Jesus.

3. Giving must be according to our means

Often the figure of ten per cent is mentioned as the amount which should be laid aside, as, it is argued, under the Law this was what was expected. This, however, is not so. The tithe was the responsibility of all, but above that there were many other opportunities to give, such as a burnt offering (the best of the herd or flock), and the vows of Leviticus 27 in which persons or possessions could be given to the Lord. The faithful who loved Jehovah could give much more than ten per cent. How much then should I give? "As God hath prospered", is the answer of Paul. In early life, particularly when newly married, we find that resources can often be stretched. A good principle is still to seek to live within our income and resist the temptation to become overburdened financially. As we consider "how much", we must be before God to weigh up all the issues and to determine in His presence the amount we will lay aside. Make the habit of giving one of the great foundations on which you build your life. Read 2 Corinthians 8.1-9 and note three encouragements to give.

1. The example of others

The churches of Macedonia are cited as an example of others who were giving. The circumstances in which they found themselves did not appear to encourage giving for they were in times of affliction and poverty, but still they laid something aside for the poor saints. So great was their desire that they had far exceeded what Paul had expected of them. What was the secret of their power? Was it not that they had first given themselves unto the Lord, and with the Lord put first all else was in place? Probably few of the Macedonians had ever met these saints from Jerusalem, but that was no barrier to them. Learn also from this the power of example! What we do influences others who are carefully observing us. Let them see that discipleship works!

2. The proof of our love

How can we express our love in an open way? To saints in need it is encouraging to know that we have a love for them, but it is of little practical value if this is not followed by action. Loving and giving are linked in Scripture, for "the Son of God...loved me, and gave himself for me" (Gal 2.20). It is only by this means that our love can be proved.

3. The example of the Lord Jesus

This is the greatest encouragement of all. He was rich before

He came to earth, with riches far beyond anything we could imagine, but as a deliberate act of His will He became poor. Compared to what was His in eternity He became poor; compared even to others on earth, He became poor. Not to the palaces of men, not to the wealth of men, but to the lowly circumstances of Nazareth He came. His was the greatest act of giving ever, never to be repeated by another, and at Calvary we see the greatest sacrifice ever. If He had not given freely we would never have known salvation. Giving lies at the very root of our redemption. If we would be like Christ we have this example to follow!

In 2 Corinthians 8 and 9 we are provided with some solid advice on how to give.

1. Resolve and action must go together (8.11)

So often we will find that we have a will to give, but never seem to get round to carrying out our purpose. We find ourselves wondering whether we can afford this, or whether our original determination was of God. The longer we wait, the less likely it is that we will ever give what we had decided. If the Lord has laid on your heart to give, perform the doing of it and do not allow delay or sloth to stop you.

2. Give out of what you have (8.11)

When there is a willing mind we feel that we would like to give more than is in our power. We look at the need and consider our contribution to be so small. Do not let this put us off. Giving to God is not measured according to the size of the need which is to be met: it is measured according to what we have. The important factor is that there first should be a willing mind. All that we have has come from God and He does not expect us to give to others what He has not given us. Give according to the resources you have even although this may seem so insignificant. The widow's mite to some appeared to be almost nothing, but its true value was recorded in heaven (Mk 12.41-44).

3. Give to ensure equality (8.14-15)

The exhortation given by Paul was not to place a burden on the Corinthians and make life easy for others. It was that the need of others should be met by those who were not in want. Later, should those who had given find themselves in want, they would have this met from those who had been the recipients of their bounty in earlier years. At the time of writing the need was in Jerusalem; in later years it could be in Corinth. Is this not further evidence that "whatsoever a man soweth, that shall he also reap" (Gal 6.7)? If we meet the need of others, our own need will be met. Dare we then hold back?

4. Give with the correct attitude (9.6-7)

Bountifully, not sparingly, is the key! If the farmer sows seed sparingly there will be no great harvest, but if he sows bountifully there will be a plentiful harvest. So it is with our giving. It must be done bountifully, without holding back, and not sparingly, only releasing the minimum. The farmer does not hold on to his seed, reluctant to sow it, for he looks beyond the sowing to the harvest and knows the link between the two. In a similar way the believer looks beyond the initial act of giving to the day of harvest. Do not look at your situation and decide how little you can give, or what is the lowest amount acceptable under the circumstances. Approach the issues with an open bountiful spirit and God will bless your desire to give as He has laid on your heart. Meanness of mind and smallness of vision are poor characteristics for a believer.

Purposefully, not haphazardly, is the way to give. We saw earlier that we give as God has prospered us, and now we learn that it is as we purpose in our heart. We must be before God and come to a determination of what He would have us give. It is a good exercise to make a covenant with God and carry this out with a faithful spirit. Giving is not done in a mindless way with little serious consideration and little prayerful thought.

Cheerfully, not grudgingly, is what God expects. The grudging giver is sorrowful at losing what he regards as his. He thinks of what he could have done with the money and considers he is the poorer by giving. He gives out of compulsion and not from a willing heart. What a sad way to follow the Lord Jesus. The cheerful giver thinks none of these things, but, under no compulsion whatsoever, he gives what he has purposed, knowing that what he is doing is bringing pleasure to God for "God loveth a cheerful giver".

What kind of givers are we! Look at the example of Barnabas who sold land and brought the proceeds to the apostles (Acts 4.36-37). Only two verses are needed to tell us the story. There was a single-minded determination to do, and it was accomplished with due dispatch. How different from Ananias and Sapphira. They wished to have the credit without the sacrifice, and what sad reading is the account of their end.

5. Give, understanding who benefits (9.8-10)
We would expect the recipient of the gift to be the first mentioned as the beneficiary of an act of bounty, but look at these verses! We have seen in v.6 that it is the sower who reaps the harvest, and in v.8 we learn that the giver will have all sufficiency in all things to enable every good work to abound. So the first named beneficiary is not the recipient, who undoubtedly *is* benefited, but the giver. How strange are the ways of God. The same principle can be seen in Philippians 4. We often rely on the promise in v.19 that God will supply all our need, but how often do we read the background to this lovely pledge. The Philippians had sent a gift to Paul on more than one occasion, the latest having been received when Epaphroditus arrived in Rome. Because they had been so bountiful Paul knew his God well enough to state without reservation that all their need would be met. If we would lean on the same promise we must fulfil the same conditions and give as bountifully as did they.

6. Give, knowing the effect produced (9.11-15)
The immediate effect was the alleviation of the need of the poor saints, but something even greater was produced in their giving of thanks to God as they recognised that a higher hand

was at work. As they considered what had been received they glorified God. How we would like to produce such a response from our actions! But how can God be glorified? Surely by there coming from our hearts a greater appreciation of the greatest gift ever given, the unspeakable, indescribable gift, the gift of the Lord Jesus Christ, so great that it is inexpressible. May the result of our giving be that many glorify God and say, "Thanks be unto God for His unspeakable gift!".

CHAPTER 12

What about Holiness?

Holiness! Does the very word make you draw back? What do you think of when you consider it? Perhaps it fills your mind with thoughts of some aged recluse, living a lonely life of prayer and meditation. To some young people it brings to mind visions of older believers hopelessly out of touch with life today, and constantly frowning on every activity that creates joy and laughter. Have you before you the thought of some self-righteous zealot who constantly criticises the behaviour of others and considers himself to be on a higher spiritual plane? Does it fill your mind with a picture of living in "No" land where negatives are the order of the day, or do you see it simply as a standard of behaviour to which you can never attain? If any one of these is your concept of holiness you are completely out of touch with what the Bible has to say.

How then do we define holiness? It is separation from evil, from everything that is not in accord with the character of God. The first lesson to learn is that God is holy. In 1 Peter 1.15-16 this point is emphasised as the foundation on which our conduct should be built. If we love God we will love holiness. There is therefore nothing mystical about this, for a desire to lead a holy life is simply a desire to live a life separate from what is evil. It is here that we discover the very first desire of God for those whom He has redeemed. Not that we should be great preachers, great personal workers, or great teachers, but primarily that we should be holy. Without that desire we have missed the main point of salvation. Remember that we have been called to be saints, to be holy ones (1 Cor 1.2). The question, however, is that if God has called us to be this, how do we put it into practice?

Paul exhorts us to "cleanse ourselves from all filthiness of the flesh and spirit, perfecting holiness in the fear of God" (2 Cor 7.1). Here we have good advice, and note that even Paul included himself in the exhortation. This verse is the closing call in the section which has dealt with the subject of the unequal yoke with unbelievers. We are taught to cleanse ourselves externally (the flesh) and internally (the spirit) from all filthiness, that is, from all that contaminates. A believer who desires fellowship with God can quickly discern contaminating influences. Conversation that is unseemly, the company of those who have no interest in the things of the Lord Jesus, listening to, watching, or even reading of behaviour or language which we would shun ourselves - all this contaminates and leaves its mark on us. Scripture does teach us that we will rub shoulders with the world, and for us that may be at school, at college, or at work, where we should seek to commend the gospel by our lives. We are faced with choices - of friends, of how we spend our time, of what we read, and of so many other issues. Make sure that you never yoke yourself with unbelievers, in marriage, in business partnerships, in politics, in social activities. Such yokes will pull you into ways that will cause you grief and diminish any desire to live a holy life. Remember that even although you may not regard yourself as "yoked" you may still come under these influences.

At the beginning of each day pray that your life might be holy and that you will be able to resist the temptations placed in front of you. You will find that the Adversary works in a very subtle way. The world teaches that an action is wrong if it harms someone else. God is left out of the calculation. Perhaps a situation may arise where you can make things easy for yourself by telling a lie, and it appears to you that no one will ever know and no one will be harmed. But you know that this is not the way of holiness. Again, you may have opportunity to take something to which you are not entitled and no one will ever be aware of the loss. Holiness, however, is incompatible with this. Should you succumb, the Holy Spirit is grieved. The desire to please God must be greater than the desire to take the easy or seemingly profitable path.

If that is the negative side we must consider the positive. Paul tells us why we should stay clear of contamination. It is to leave the way open for us to perfect holiness in the fear of God. To perfect holiness is to see it increasing daily in our lives, to see it growing and becoming our standard of behaviour in everything. Go in for actions and activities which you know are pleasing to Him. We please Him by not becoming enmeshed in the world and therefore leaving ourselves free to direct our energies to the work of God (2 Tim 2.4). We do well to take note that obedience to parents is noted as being pleasing to the Lord (Col 3.20). Keeping His commandments leads to our doing those things that are pleasing in His sight (1 Jn 3.22). How much of your life must be lived in this way? All of it! "Be ye holy in all manner of conversation" (1 Pet 1.15) teaches us that God intends every part of our lives to be included. If we would present our bodies to Him they must be holy (Rom 12.1). Prayer must be marked by holy hands (1 Tim 2.8). Men can be holy (2 Pet 1.21), as can women (1 Pet 3.5).

Behind this desire for holiness there is a fear of God. This fear is not one of terror, but of reverential awe. It is awareness of the greatness of God, a realisation of all that is enjoyed by acting in accord with His will, and of what can be lost through acting contrary to it. Bring the fear of God into every consideration and determine to please Him in all that you do. The blessings now are incalculable.

We can therefore see that holiness, rather than being some mystical higher plain on which a few live, is very practical and involves every believer. Go in for it and make it your ambition to see it working out as each day passes. In His Kingdom it will mark everything, in the houses, in the streets, and in the temple (Zech 14.20-21). Let us ensure that we make it a reality now.

CHAPTER 13

What about Gossip?

The work for God was going well. Along the way there had been problems, but, although there was still much to do, there was enough evidence to let all see that God was working through His people. There was plenty to give thanks for in that, you may say. In the background, however, one individual was doing his utmost to ensure that Nehemiah's work was halted (Neh 6.1-9). Gashmu, the rumourmonger, the talebearer, was hard at work spreading his poisonous gossip, which, like all gossip, took a true fact, embellished it, and built on it until it was beyond all recognition. So Gashmu, the father of all talebearers, displays the features common to those who follow his footsteps, seeking to harm by bending truth until it is lies, and seeking to destroy without having the courage to face the victim. Sad to say, modern Gashmus are alive and thriving, and we would do well to consider how they work and what our response to them must be.

When you are in the company of believers there are often stories told which concern others not present. In some cases these are complimentary and in some cases they are amusing and completely harmless (although be careful that these are not exaggerated to become amusing). Always be on your guard and, as a general rule, never speak about someone unless it is to say something that would still be said if they were present. Gossips will soon make themselves known and when they speak, remember how damaging they are.

The first thing to note is that gossip is harmful. One of the least attractive personalities presented to us in the book of

Proverbs is the talebearer. Twice over we are told of the harmful effects of his conduct. "The words of the talebearer are as wounds" (18.8; 26.22). Wounds hurt and weaken the victim, and what may appear to be innocent chatter can have lethal results, your words being used as the weapon to inflict damage.

Note, secondly, that gossip is contentious. Proverbs 26.20 tells us that the talebearer is the cause of strife. How many problems have been created by the spreading of unfounded rumours which seem to turn into confirmed facts with the many tellings of the story. If you are ever tempted to pass on some little anecdote, consider the effect this would have if it were to come to the ears of the one whom it concerns. How much trouble could it cause!

So, if strife and hurt are the results of the spreading of gossip, let us now consider the cause of this conduct. One prime cause is jealousy. You may know someone whom you consider to overshadow you in some way. Do they have a better job? Is he a brother who perhaps has a spiritual gift which you desire to have, or is it simply that he or she is carrying on a work for God which causes you to be envious? A few words can soon create questions in the minds of others. You can use words with double meaning, or even speak as if you had a genuine care for the person of whom you are speaking. You are only mentioning this, after all, because you are concerned. Equally effective is the ploy of only telling a part of a story and thus casting a very different light on an incident than that which truth would reveal. Adding to or taking away from the truth is not only forbidden in the handling of Scripture, it is dangerous in any matter. Paul was at the receiving end of this kind of behaviour. In Romans 3.8 we learn that some were speaking in a slanderous way of his teaching, and he had to refute these false accusations.

Another easily identifiable cause is immaturity. How we love to know something that others do not know, and how we enjoy being the centre of attention as we tell our story. In order to hold the interest of everyone we add just a little emphasis to a particular point or even add another "fact" to make the story more enthralling. Where the information is true but confidential we have no right to reveal it; Proverbs again warns us that the talebearer reveals secrets (20.19). This is a serious breach of trust.

Idleness also plays its part. In 1 Timothy 5.13 Paul warns young widows against becoming busybodies. The danger of going from house to house, with little to do to fill the day, gives rise to a situation where we learn something in one house which becomes the subject of conversation in another. Often under the guise of having a concern for the well-being of others, such characters, we find, can leave havoc in their wake. Experience has proved that being a busybody is not confined to young widows. Brethren and sisters, old and young, can all fall into this trap!

Boosting your own ego is also what causes many a story to be told. You make your subject that bit blacker in order to show how faithful was your defence of truth. In so doing, often the answers which you say you gave are those which later reflection brought to your mind rather than those which you gave at the time.

If you know of something in the life of a believer which requires action, verify the facts thoroughly and then speak to him or her, and, if necessary, to the elders of the assembly. There are clearly laid down Scriptural procedures for handling such difficulties, and gossiping simply compounds the problem.

How then do we react to the talebearer? Proverbs 20.19 tells us not to meddle with him. Even if he flatters you he will speak to others about you, just as he speaks to you about others, so do not seek much of his company. And what do we do when we are in a crowd where gossip is being traded? The challenge is there presented to us to ensure that the conversation is guided back to safe ground and to show that you will not allow that line of talk to continue.

In any conversation we do well to remember the words of Colossians 4.6: "Let your speech be alway with grace, seasoned with salt". Words used ill-advisedly are like a fire which runs out of control and we have little idea of the ultimate damage which can be caused (Jas 3.5). Let us ensure that verbal fire-raising is something with which we can never be charged.

CHAPTER 14

What about Temptation?

The problem of temptation is one which every believer encounters. With some it produces a feeling of hopelessness and discouragement, a sense that their spiritual life must be at a low ebb if such feelings occur. But does Scripture teach this? How are we told to handle temptation?

It is worth re-stating that all believers experience temptation. This is not an indication that we are out of touch with God. Satan may offer a suggestion, but only when it becomes our desire and we translate it into action, does it become sin. Remember the great example of the Lord Jesus who endured temptations before the commencement of His public ministry. Never think that the Lord Jesus could have sinned, for "God cannot be tempted of evil" (Jas 1.13), and, "Whosoever is born of God doth not commit sin" (1 Jn 3.9). These temptations were a means of displaying His sinlessness. But note that Satan knows no bounds as to whom he will attack.

God tests us, but never tempts us - see again James 1.13. Often in the midst of a test we will be tempted by the wiles of the Devil, in his providing a way out which looks attractive, but which we know is sinful. Many a believer in straitened circumstances has had the opportunity of solving the problem by taking something which was not his to have, or by entering employment which is incompatible with the Lordship of Christ.

How then does temptation work? James spells this out. We are "drawn away of (our) own lust, and enticed" (1.14). There still is in us that which could respond to any prompting to disobey God, desires which must be kept under control if we wish to live a holy life. Temptation seeks to activate these desires by offering what is, firstly, attractive: the easy way out, the solution to a long-standing problem, the fulfilment of some desire which we have been unable to satisfy. We are never offered an unattractive temptation. The well-watered plains looked enticing to Lot; Bathsheba appeared attractive to David; telling untruths looked an easy way out of a difficulty for Peter; and, of course, the promise "ye shall be as gods" overwhelmed Eve.

Some temptations are easier to spot than others. In moral matters the issues are clear, but on occasions when we are faced with decisions we have to discern whether or not an apparent solution is merely a way of disobedience. The pathway of obedience does not always follow the apparently attractive route.

Temptation is also deceptive. When James speaks of our being enticed he is using a word which has the idea of bait, and bait serves two important purposes. It is made up of something which looks attractive to the victim, thus drawing the victim towards it. It also disguises the hook or the trap which is in place, the victim only realising the danger when it is too late and the lure has been taken. Thus it is with temptation. The true nature of what is offered is hidden to us until we have succumbed, and we learn that what appeared so attractive and desirable has a concealed hook which catches us. He who is aware of the true nature of the bait will avoid it. He who is not aware and who allows his desires to be translated into action will learn of the cost when the sin has been committed.

When faced with these issues do not be allured by the apparent excitement and enjoyment which is offered, but rather look beyond this to the cost. Ask the question, "What happens after?". Be spiritually intelligent therefore and do not swallow the bait. Sin, when it is finished, brings forth death (Jas 1.15); no good can come of it, and further difficulties are always the result.

How, then, should we handle temptation? A prime lesson

is to avoid every situation which would put temptation in your way. If Peter had never stood in bad company at the fire! If David had never been on the housetop! At work or even at school there is always the temptation to conform to the conduct of our colleagues, so, spending leisure time with those who are not believers is a potential source of temptation. You know your own weakness, so think ahead! So many of the temptations to which we fall prey occur at those periods when we are not busy and have time on our hands. Sad to say you may even find yourself in the company of other believers, but still in places that are dangerous. Determine therefore to use your time in a spiritually profitable way. Pray about what your intentions for the day are and you will know when to say, "No"!

Learn, second, to use the Scriptures, the main weapon we have in this battle. A soldier becomes familiar with his weapon long before he has to use it in earnest. He does not stand in the midst of the battle thumbing his way through a *How to use a rifle* manual. The enemy would see to it that he did not get beyond page one. No, by reading the manual prior to the battle, and by constant practice, he knows his weapon and is ready to use it immediately it is needed. So it is with the Scriptures. Read them, put them into practice, become familiar with handling them, and when Satan calls you will be able to resist with the intelligent use of Scripture. The sword of the Spirit is the Word of God (Eph 6.17), that is, the verse or passage for that particular moment, the Word which, because of your prior study of Scripture is familiar to you and can be used swiftly in your own defence. Follow the example of the great Teacher who said over and over again, "It is written...".

Remember, third, that there is a way of escape from every temptation. Read 1 Corinthians 10.13 and you will learn that no temptation is so great that falling into it is inevitable. Each time you are tempted God provides the way of escape which is especially suited to meet the temptation. Look, therefore, for this, and take it immediately. To delay may bring disaster. You will never be able to say, "There was nothing I could do about it". There always is something you can do, but have you the spiritual will to respond to God's provision of the way of escape?

Resist the devil, live as an overcomer, make each temptation a victory, and gain strength and encouragement for whatever lies ahead.

CHAPTER 15

What about Backsliding?

As the apostle Paul is preparing to come to the end of his service on earth there takes place in Rome one of the saddest farewells recorded in Scripture (2 Tim 4.10). Demas, who has been a fellow worker with Paul, intimates his intention to leave Paul in Rome and make his way to Thessalonica. We do not know what reasons were given for this journey, but the apostle is able to discern what is in Demas' heart. We learn that it is a love for this present world which has caused him to abandon the apostle. Sad to say, our last view of Demas is of a backslider leaving the pathway of service, perhaps for the pathway of pleasure.

It is true that we all can remember times in our Christian lives when our spiritual desires were weak, but a backslider is one who deliberately turns his back on a life of serving the Master to pursue his own course in association with the world. A backslider is a believer who thinks as the world thinks and ultimately lives according to the world's principles. Some in this condition leave the fellowship of their local assembly, but some never do, seeking to keep a foot in both camps. The condition is one of such sadness that we have to ask what causes it and enquire if it is possible for a backslider to be restored to useful service.

The prodigal son (Lk 15.11-32) is often rightly used in the gospel as a picture of the sinner, but he is also a picture of one who has turned his back on God after enjoying the benefits of relationship with Him. As with Demas, it was the lure of the far country, the lure of the world, which caused him to go astray.

This highlights one of the main causes of backsliding in the lives of young believers. The world looks attractive, and the Christian life appears restrictive, so we decide to sample the pleasures that we see around us.

Gehazi, the servant of Elisha, ended his days in the palace of the king, but at what a cost (2 Kings 8.4). His downfall was his love of money, and to acquire it he destroyed his testimony and condemned himself and his family to the scourge of leprosy (2 Kings 5.20-27). Does he not have a message for us in our materialistic society?

Lot looked on the well-watered plains of Jordan and choose a life of ease rather than the pathway of the pilgrim (Gen 13.10-11). Some still follow his example and turn back when they meet the rigours of service.

Samson succumbed to the beguiling allurements of a godless woman and destroyed his power for God (Judg 16.4-5).

Elimelech, faced with the difficulty of famine, took his family with him to Moab, thus teaching us that we may take others with us on this downward journey (Ruth 1.2).

And so today Satan's methods have not changed. The attraction of the world, the love of money, the call to a life of ease, the difficulties of testimony, the attraction of an unsaved friend, or even simple spiritual lethargy still take their toll and cause Christians to become backslidden in heart. It is a feature of this condition that many who find themselves in it blame others for their state, but by this they merely acknowledge that their lives are not as they should be. Note that good company is no guarantee that we are immune. No better company was available than that enjoyed by Demas, and Gehazi had years with Elisha behind him.

Why is it then that we are led astray like this? The seeds of it are sown long before it grows and becomes visible. Backsliding is, first, a heart condition. Like so many diseases its symptoms do not become obvious until it has been present for some time. We go to meetings, but our interests lie elsewhere; we sit in conferences, but our minds are far away; we participate in the Breaking of Bread, but our contributions are old and stale. We know how we are, although even our loved ones and the other saints in the assembly are unaware of it. Beware if you can discern in your own heart the early symptoms of backsliding.

But let us go a little deeper and ask why it is that our desire for spiritual things decreases and allows Satan to introduce other interests into our lives. Surely the main reason is that we neglect the Scriptures and the daily need for prayer. It is our responsibility to keep in touch with God, and if we do so the resources are at our disposal to ensure that we are preserved from wandering. If we give attention to the vital things of Christian living, we will find that that kind of life has far greater attraction and satisfaction than anything found in the world. God has not saved us to give us a less desireable, less joyful, less satisfying life than that experienced by those who reject Him. For the believer He has provided the best, and it is ours to go in for it to the full.

If you are in this sad, worldly condition you may wonder if there is a way back. Take heart from the fact that the prodigal came home and that Naomi returned from Moab. So, restoration is possible, but you have to take the decisive steps which lead to this. That poor man, the prodigal son, sitting among the swine confessed his sin and decisively stated, "I will arise and go to my father" (Lk 15.18). Of Naomi it is written that "she arose...that she might return from the country of Moab" (Ruth 1.6). It may be that your life while you were away in the far country created problems which have to be faced up to, but without that determination to return you will never again know the joy of close daily fellowship with the Master.

If you do not take this step the outlook is not good. There is no example in Scripture of anyone turning back from discipleship and prospering in the things which really matter. God's ways with us are often perplexing, but they always work out in accordance with His Word. You may consider yourself to be immune, that you have your life well under control, but loss of well-being, of joy, of satisfaction, and of possessions were all the experience of those in Scripture who sought to live away from God.

So note the word of warning. Are you living as a Christian with heart affections elsewhere? Take decisive action before it is too late. Are you further down the backslider's pathway? Determine to return today. Go into the presence of God and confess your condition, asking for His help to come back. Life is too short and the opportunities for service pass too quickly to squander our days living a life producing nothing that will find His approval at the Judgment Seat. We owe it to ourselves, to our loved ones, to our fellow believers, and, above all, to the Lord.

CHAPTER 16

What about my Employment?

Whether you are at school, in further education, or have a job, the days for many of us from Monday to Friday are occupied with what we call our "secular employment". To some of us this is a time when we enjoy what we do and are happy to leave home every morning to set about the business of the day. To others, however, the days are far from enjoyable and are regarded as hours to be tolerated. The quicker they are over the better so that they can return to doing what they really enjoy. No matter what our attitude is, employment has one thing in common for us all: it probably is when we are in touch with unbelievers to a greater extent than at any other time. If we look at it this way it can change our approach to our employment and help us to regard it, not simply as a boring grind, but as a unique opportunity to live for God.

In the teaching given to slaves, the Bible has clear instructions for us regarding how to behave in this environment. You may argue that the days of slavery have passed, but in the society of New Testament times slaves were an accepted part of the working population, so the teaching given to them in Scripture is of more than passing interest to employees today.

To start with, observe that you must show respect to your employer at all times (1 Tim 6.1). We speak about those who "deserve our respect" but here we are told to show unconditional respect to those who are our superiors. Should you fail to do this "the name of God and his doctrine (are) blasphemed". The unbeliever sees you as a representative of your God, and by your behaviour the name of God is brought into disrepute. In handling your employer's matters you must show that you are trustworthy and not one given to purloining, to keeping for yourself part of what has been committed to your care (Tit 2.10).

There will often be occasions when it is possible to obtain something as a "perk". This can be an awkward situation, especially if you are one of a group of employees who regularly avail themselves of this "perk" and feel that, by refusing, you are putting them in danger of discovery. Much wisdom is required in this, but never compromise your position by accepting what you know is not your due. Do it once and your testimony falls.

Should your employer be a believer, do not expect privileges from him which are not given to others. You may also feel that you can be more familiar with him because he is a brother in the Lord, but the spiritual relationship which you have does not give you social equality. The business relationship must be honoured, and although when gathering in the assembly you can treat him as a brother (if older than you, with the respect due to one who is older), back at work he is still the master.

In addition to this the believer must not be known as one who is constantly complaining, grumbling, and contradicting. We have all known employees who are first to voice their grievances, who become leaders of the disaffected, and who are well known as the spokespersons for the unhappy. No claim that you are looking after the interests of others will justify the damage to your testimony through such an attitude. Much better to "adorn the doctrine of God our Saviour in all things" (Tit 2.10). Let those who work with you see in you a demeanour which enhances what you believe, showing a beautiful example of your faith in action. Unbelievers will never have opportunities like this elsewhere to observe at close range how a Christian reacts under the strain and pressures of daily life. Show them that you are different and that Christian life is attractive.

In this context a further danger is highlighted in Colossians 3.22. It is possible that you simply serve with "eyeservice", that is, you seek to please your employer only when you are being watched. When you are unobserved your duties are neglected or carried out in a careless way, but when you are seen you become the most efficient worker around. If you are conscious of the fact that God sees all, you will quickly learn that it is what He sees and not what men see that is important.

What you must keep before you is that at work, as at every other time, you are serving the Lord Christ. A Monday is every bit as much occupied with the Lord's service as a Lord's Day. We have misused the expression "Lord's service" as if it only applied to the work we do directly for the assembly, but it is far wider than this: it relates to everything you do every day of your life. Willingness and a pleasing manner must be ours whether in the company of the world at work or in the company of Christians in the assembly - "whatsoever ye do, do it heartily, as to the Lord, and not unto men" (Col 3.23).

In your desire to do well do not forget your spiritual responsibilities. Should a new position be offered to you, consider the spiritual issues most carefully. If acceptance means that you will miss many meetings, do you really need to accept? There are many who through shift work have little choice in this matter, but if possible it would be better to avoid a job which will force you to be absent from the gatherings of the assembly on a regular basis. The same considerations must be taken into account when you move to another area. Again this can be thrust upon you with no opportunity to say, "No", particularly in these times, but if you willingly pursue a position in an area where there is no assembly testimony, are you really doing it because you wish to evangelise that area, or is money and promotion your real motive?

Always beware lest the love of money becomes the driving force. You have to work, indeed to refuse to do so is contrary to Scripture (2 Thess 3.10), but remember that the purpose is to meet your own needs and to distribute to others. A graphic picture is drawn in 1 Timothy 6.9-10 of one who becomes prey to the love of money. He falls into a temptation which he is sure he can control, but this quickly becomes a snare from which he cannot free himself. He then finds that he is feeling the hurt of it, and sadly he is finally overcome, drowned in "destruction and perdition", suffering loss for time and eternity. How many have been ensnared in this way in their desire to get on and be successful! God makes some rich, but to make this objective your avowed intention is to court disaster.

One final word to those who are about to start work or go to college. You may wonder how you will tell people that you are a Christian. The best way is to make it known in a quiet way at the beginning. When your colleagues ask you to socialise with them you will find that they really do not expect, nor want, a Christian to accompany them. Say, "No", once and you will have little trouble in future.

Five days a week, rubbing shoulders with unbelievers, and you say there are few openings for the gospel today? You cannot use your employer's hours to stand in the office or factory and preach, but you can, with far greater effectiveness, be a living sermon, preaching Christ by your manner of life. Do not waste the opportunity.

CHAPTER 17

What about my Social Life?

One of the main differences between your life as a young believer today in Britain and that known to previous generations is the amount of free time which you now enjoy and the money which you have available. In common with the rest of society your standards of pay and conditions have improved greatly. Who now pays his employer for the privilege of being an apprentice? Even the impoverished student has known harder times.

In a sense this has presented you with difficulties which your parents never had to face. Without time or money, there was never the question of going to places which were regarded as "worldly". Cars were for the privileged few and thus the issue of travelling long distances for a few hours of enjoyment never arose.

How things have changed! In the past it was accepted that Christians would not frequent bars and public houses, but society's drive to make these more respectable has made them perhaps more acceptable to believers. The media in all its forms has also increased interest in the entertainment world and provided the means for the home to be a place in which we can engage in a wide range of pastimes which would have been beyond belief to our grandparents.

So how do we act in the affluent society of today? A quick look round most assemblies shows that few of the young display many signs of straitened circumstances. So many pleasures and opportunities for enjoyment beckon and, if older brethren and sisters frown on some of these activities, are they not simply old-fashioned and unwilling to accept that times have changed? Surely there is nothing wrong with enjoying yourself while you are young? You have a social life which they never had, and therefore they cannot be expected to understand it.

Young people have energy which has to be expended, but how do you discern what is and what is not profitable for you? You may like sport, but what company does that lead you into? You may have a particular hobby, but is it a help to your spiritual life? How does a young believer decide how to spend his free time?

We must keep in mind that there are activities which hinder spiritual life. Time is precious, and to waste it by being occupied with the entertainment of the world will not promote spiritual growth. Does television constantly draw you? Are you addicted to the Internet? Do you find Saturday sporting events irresistible? Do you spend your free time in the company of unbelievers? All this leaves you open to the danger of filling your mind with language and behaviour which is unseemly. Is a Saturday night occupied like this a good means of preparing for the Lord's Day? At the end of any time passed in that way do you not feel a sense of waste, of disappointment with yourself, of failure? About any interests which you have, ask one question: not, "What is wrong with it?", but rather, "What is in it for God?"

How then can spare time be spent? It is vital to put God first in seeking to please Him. "Do all to the glory of God" (1 Cor 10.31), is advice which we would do well to heed, but what does it mean practically? Vine describes "the glory of God" as "the manifestation of His character and acts". Thus it is to be "followers (or, imitators) of God" (Eph 5.1). Ask yourself, therefore, the questions: "Can I manifest God's character in what I am doing? Can I be an imitator of God here?" Ensure also, that you do nothing which will deprive you of the privilege of being able to testify to those who are unbelievers. You will find, when you seek to speak to them of the gospel, that they have long memories.

But you say, "There are things which I like to do and which I feel quite free to do, and although others are offended by them, I cannot see how they are dishonouring to God. As a believer am I not free to go by my own conscience?" We do not, however, live to ourselves. "Take heed lest by any means this liberty of yours become a stumblingblock to them that are weak" (1 Cor 8.9). If you insist on continuing the practices which offend others you may be the means of causing your brother to stumble and fall. For example, at lunch time you may accompany your colleagues to a public house. You do not touch alcohol and only have a sandwich. A believer sees you and is deeply offended, but Satan soon uses this to impress on him that he is too extreme in his views and should mix a little more. He yields, finds the pull of alcohol too great, and so his testimony is destroyed. The seriousness of being the cause of such a disaster is emphasised in 1 Corinthians 8.12 when we learn that such conduct is sinning against Christ. How careful we must be in what we do as others are watching us.

Stewardship of your resources also comes into this. Are you spending the money which has been given you in a God honouring way? Compared to what you give to the Lord on a Lord's Day, how much do you spend on socialising? You are not expected to live your life in a vacuum, for God has a way of life for you which is far more rewarding, enjoyable, and satisfying than anything which is to be found in the world. The company of other young believers who have an interest in spiritual things is of prime importance. This is not to suggest that every spare moment must be occupied with Bible study (that will nevertheless be an important part of every day), but you will be preserved from much of the temptation which lies in wait for those who go in for the company of the world. Apart from this, the fellowship and friendship of other believers is something which can be fulfilling and satisfying. Paul looked forward to meeting the Roman believers (Rom 15.24) and to being "somewhat filled" with their company. You will find that the company of other believers can be encouraging and instructive, and that even casual conversations on matters of common interest can teach us lessons which will be useful in the future.

Make it your practice to attend conferences and ministry meetings whenever possible. How can you become well-taught if you ignore the teachers? It is not clever or mature to disparage those who attend such meetings, or the older believers who arrange them. There are areas of the country where most Saturday evenings present you with a selection of meetings, so do not forego this privilege, for others would give much to have such a rich choice.

What about work in the gospel? Have you considered engaging in tracting or open air work (in the correct location). If you are looking for something to do there is plenty of scope and no need to be idle. Our social life is no different from other areas of life; it has to be used wisely in the service of Christ. When we are young, how we use these hours is a good indication of where our heart lies, and a good pointer to how our lives will develop. It is necessary to be in certain places at work or college, we feel we have to be at the regular assembly meetings, but in our spare time we are free to choose how we occupy ourselves, and that is the test of our interests. What does your social life tell others about you?

CHAPTER 18

What about Politics?

Every generation sees around it the seeming injustices of life and the problems which are faced by the poor, the unemployed, the weak, and the elderly. Christians particularly should be keenly aware of the difficulties which confront so many. As young believers survey the sad conditions of their society they may wonder at times whether the political arena is one in which it is worth becoming involved in order to help to better the conditions of those around them.

Further impetus may be given to this way of thinking by looking upward at those who are in authority, and becoming aware of the lack of righteousness in their lives. Entrance into politics may seem an attractive route, introducing Christian principles into the decision-making processes of the government of the day. The world itself looks favourably upon such an involvement, although it prefers that the subject of personal morality and righteousness of conduct be left out of the manifesto. "Christian" movements, the purpose of which is to address areas of need in society, are usually welcomed.

Paul deals with the involvement of the believer with the government of the day in Romans 13. Keep in mind as you read this chapter that the Caesar who held sway when these words were written, Nero by name, was a cruel murderer. The Roman Empire was populated by many whose lives were subject to the most unjust restrictions, and whose future was often held in the hands of men who cared little for their well-being. It was a society which had no shortage of good causes to espouse.

As far as the government is concerned we are told that as believers we must be obedient citizens, and three reasons are given to back this up. The first four verses of the chapter show that government is ordained of God to be a terror to those who carry out evil deeds. It is therefore in place to preserve law and order by praising the one who does well and by punishing the one who commits evil. When a government acts in a way which is contrary to the Word of God we are told that we should obey God rather than men, but this does not extend to seeking to overthrow the government. The believer in this situation will order his conduct according to his conscience.

The second reason is our conscience. The opening section has taught us that there should be no open uprising against civil authority. Here we are instructed that there should be no private rebellion. This may take the form of refusing to pay taxes, and any other levies, which are claimed by the state. Should this be our practice our consciences are affected. The question of whether we approve of the use to which our taxes are put is not a point at issue. We must pay, no matter what we feel about the spending programme of the government. Where we are employees, the employer normally takes care of our tax liabilities by deducting them from our gross wage. Where we are self-employed the whole responsibility rests on our shoulders and any temptation to avoid paying our dues must be firmly resisted.

In dealing with this subject Paul introduces another debt which we must discharge. The display of love is something which we must all show, and, indeed, the responsibilities of a citizen are summed up in the Law, and set out in v.9. The regulation of our conduct by this standard is a real contribution which we can make to our society.

The third reason presented to us is the nature of the times in which we live. The fact that the day of our salvation is nearer than when we believed will affect the manner of our lives. We are conscious of the shortness of time and of the need to use every moment in a way that is of eternal value. We are living in a world that has rebelled against the government of God, but we are looking to the day when that rebellion will be over. The conditions which cause so much pain and despair in the world around us will be eliminated when He comes to establish His righteous rule.

In the light of the teaching of this chapter, should we become involved in the political issues of the day? Is it not noteworthy that in this section of the epistle, dealing with our relationship to civil authority, there is no plea to become so involved? How then can we help in this sad world of ours? In 1 Timothy 2.2 we are exhorted to pray "for kings, and for all that are in authority". This is where we can bring our concerns to Him who is able to move amongst the councils of men. The power which is available through prayer is better far than anything which civil authority has at its disposal. Our prayers are based on the desire to lead a quiet and peaceable life in all godliness and honesty. Should rulers be saved, for that is the object of our prayer, such a condition in society would exist. Saints would be left to run their affairs as they desired.

"But", you may say, "can we not do something 'practical'?" Leaving aside the fact that prayer is extremely practical, there are other means of meeting need. Believers should be known as individuals who have a care for the needy. Our willingness to help in meeting such need will commend the gospel. Remember, however, that we have to do good to all men, but "especially unto them who are of the household of faith" (Gal 6.10).

Having known salvation we now are pilgrims moving towards another destination, and are strangers in a land which is not our home. The task which falls to us is to preach the gospel and to display the Lord Jesus to a world lost in sin. Great though the issues of the day may be, there is none greater than that. Any involvement which detracts from that end is to be avoided. We have a great commission to carry out and political action can only hold us back.

CHAPTER 19

What about the Sisters?

There is in the world today a great movement promoting so called "equality" for women. The purpose of this chapter is not to examine the claims of that movement in detail, but to address two manifestations of it in assembly life.

The head-covering of sisters has been the subject of much debate. It is felt by some that the wearing of a head-covering in the gathering of the saints is an anachronism. It is, they say, a tradition that cannot be supported by Scripture and irrelevant in the days in which we live. We have heard it stated that we should be putting all our effort into evangelism and not insisting on old-fashioned customs based on prejudice that make the assembly unappealing to those who come to our gatherings.

It is true that we should not insist on perpetuating traditions which have no warrant in Scripture, but the practice of the sister covering her head, and of the brother uncovering his head, is one which can be substantiated from the Word of God. Teaching regarding this is found in 1 Corinthians 11, and it should be noted that the covered head of the woman is one of three symbols which are introduced in the chapter, the bread and the wine being the other two. We learn from this, therefore, that the issue is one of importance and not to be relegated to the role of teaching which we can embrace or ignore if we so wish. Who gave us the right to state that the second half of 1 Corinthians 11 is of greater importance than the first half?

Paul brings before us in the early verses of this chapter the divine order of headship. You may ask, "What is headship?". It is the order which God has stamped upon His creation, for order and authority mark all His work. In creation the man is the head of the woman and Christ is the Head of the man. This is an order which is denied by a world which refuses to acknowledge the fact that the Lord is Head over all, and which invariably believes that man is the supreme authority or, if not man, a god of their own creation, not the God and Father of our Lord Jesus Christ revealed in the Scriptures.

When believers gather together it will be their purpose to ensure that the divine order of headship and authority is acknowledged. The head of man is Christ and therefore the man uncovers his head, which symbolises Christ, declaring thus that He alone should be seen and His authority alone acknowledged. The woman, on the other hand, covers her head to declare that man, her head, is hidden. The seriousness of ignoring this teaching can be seen from the fact that the man who covers his head dishonours his head, thus dishonouring the Lord. The woman who refuses to cover her head puts man to shame by ignoring the divinely given order of headship.

It should be noted that the covered head of the sister is not an acknowledgement that the woman is less spiritual than the man, nor does it indicate that the woman is less well-taught in the Scriptures. Some even claim to see in the symbol a declaration of woman's inferiority, but this is not found in Scripture. The symbol is simply exhibiting an acceptance of the order of creation, with differing roles for man and woman. Both roles have dignity, and it is pleasing to God to see them acknowledged.

Another objection which is raised is that the head-covering of which 1 Corinthians speaks is the long hair of the woman. In the NIV a footnote is included which indicates this. This footnote, where it refers to v.4, gives the words "with long hair" in place of "with his head covered", thus reading: "Every man who prays or prophesies with long hair dishonours his head". The covering is therefore made to be long hair and this rendering is adhered to in the remainder of the chapter. Does this, however, stand the test of scrutiny? A closer examination of the text reveals that the word used by Paul in v.15 to describe the covering of a woman's hair is quite different from that which he uses to describe a covering placed on the head. To describe the woman's hair he speaks of a cloak, a wrap, or a mantle, but to describe the covering placed on the head he speaks of a top-covering which comes down upon the head. Quite apart from this, to believe that the covering is the hair of the woman makes nonsense of v.6, which would then mean that "If a woman has cut her hair short, or shaved it, let her have her hair cut short".

The spiritual sister reading Paul's teaching can see quite clearly the requirements which are placed upon her, and upon the brethren. Some, on the other hand, have asserted that the covering is only necessary for certain meetings of the assembly and not for them all. Gospel meetings, Bible Classes, Young People's meetings are all cited as examples of gatherings where this practice is not necessary. This shows a lack of understanding of Scripture. Wherever believers assemble together for spiritual exercise, no matter where the gathering takes place, the heads of the sisters must be covered. There are not two tiers of gatherings in Scripture, and if we desire the presence of the Lord with us we will acknowledge His authority in this way.

If you have young children you may ask whether your daughter should have a head covering when coming to the assembly gatherings. It may be true that she has not yet accepted the Saviour, and, even if she has, she may not be in fellowship in the assembly. It is wise to remember, however, that you are bringing her up to know what is involved in being a believer, and the head-covering is a part of her education.

From time to time the question arises of how large the head-covering should be. Obviously it should be large enough to cover the head, and the sister who has a desire to please the Lord will ensure that her head-covering does this. A little decorative piece of cloth perched on the top of the head and covering very little of it does not fulfil the requirements of Scripture. We must not forget 1 Corinthians 11.10 where we learn that this teaching is because of the angels. Angelic beings know well that Satan fell because he desired to overthrow divine order in creation. He sought to ascend and be like the Most High, thus usurping the authority of God. Because of this he was judged. In the viewing gallery of heaven the angels look on and they see in the gatherings of the local church the glad, willing acknowledgement by believers of the truth which Satan despised. As the saints gather, angels are being educated by seeing the effect on the lives of men and women of the grace of God in salvation. What a privilege to be part of that great work.

Another issue which has been raised is that of the silence of sisters in gatherings of the assembly. We are told that Philip the evangelist had daughters who prophesied and that 1 Corinthians 11 speaks of a woman praying or prophesying. We must, however, remember the words of the apostle Paul: "Let your women keep silence in the churches" (1 Cor 14.34), and the equally clear teaching of 1 Timothy 2.11-12.

In the case of the daughters of Philip the evangelist there is no record of them prophesying in a local church. As Scriptures do not contradict each other, Paul is not contemplating in 1 Corinthians 11.4-5 that women should pray or prophecy publicly in the gatherings of the assembly. Where he writes, "every woman that prayeth or prophesieth..." (v.5) Paul is dealing with the question of the head-covering; he is not expressing his approval of the public participation of women. He does not deal with this, and with the exercise of spiritual gift and public speaking in the assembly, until ch.14. That is why the question of the silence of sisters is left until that chapter.

In order to allow sisters to take part publicly some assemblies have resorted to discontinuing their prayer meetings, Bible teaching meetings etc., and have replaced them with house groups for this purpose. It is the responsibility of elders to ensure that meetings are convened for prayer and teaching where all the church can gather together into one place (1 Cor 11.17-20). To fail to have this carried out is to fail the assembly. An assembly divided into separate groups is not taught in the Word of God.

The question which faces a sister considering these matters is that of how important obedience to the Scriptures is in her life. Pointing to those who have adopted other practices does not take away from us the requirement to study the Word of God and to ensure that we follow the teaching in our own lives. To refuse to obey the Word of God in these important matters is evidence of a rebellious spirit. As young believers seeking to live for God we will be careful to please Him in this, as in every other issue of life.

CHAPTER 20

What about Courtship?

In the present day, marriage is under attack. Increasingly it is becoming accepted practice for two people to live together without entering into marriage, sadly evidenced by the fact that "partner" has taken the place of "husband", or "wife" in the vocabulary of the media and even in the wording of many of the forms and documents issued by the authorities. The young believer is faced with a society where casual, short-term relationships are the order of the day, and where even among those who do marry, divorce is reaching epidemic proportions.

Care must be taken that the attitudes of the world do not enter into your thinking on courtship and marriage. The choosing of a husband or wife is one of the most important decisions which you will make and must not be influenced by the practices which surround you in the world. Remember, first, that courtship is always with a view to marriage. Young men must not make up their minds to marry and then embark on a course of courting as many girls as possible until a suitable one is found. Young ladies must not seek to become the girl friends of one young man after another until this selection process is exhausted. This behaviour is not worthy of a Christian and often leads to unnecessary heartbreak when one party is seen to be insincere. Do not form attachments lightly.

With this in mind resist the pressure felt when your friends begin to pair off and you feel that something must be done because all those who are eligible will soon be unavailable. Rather make prayer the starting point. Pray that you will be led to find the husband or wife planned for you by God, and consult the Scriptures to ensure that no mistakes are made. Here are some helpful guidelines.

Never consider entering into courtship with an unbeliever. This would lead to a marriage which is contrary to the Scriptures - "Be ye not unequally yoked together with unbelievers" (2 Cor 6.14) - and thus to a deliberate act of disobedience. You may think that such a friendship is but harmless fun from which you can withdraw at any time, but beware, for attachments become very strong. You may be young, never having mixed much outside of your circle of Christian friends, and then you meet someone, perhaps at work or college, and feel an attraction grow. Possibly you are a little older and are disappointed that you have never married, so when someone comes into your life you are flattered that your feelings are being returned. No matter the circumstances, life seems to brighten, and when this attraction becomes so strong that you cannot see how it is wrong, your emotions take over completely. Before long you find that this friendship has developed to the point where it is more important to you than spiritual things. Feelings, however, are always a bad barometer of what is right and wrong and the Scriptures are the only sound guide.

If you are in this position presently please step back and break off a relationship not sanctioned by Scripture. The object of your affections may have a great personality and be kind and considerate, with many other commendable features. You may even find an excitement because that person's way of life is so different to yours. All these are, however, more than outweighed by the fact that he or she is an unbeliever. For that nothing compensates.

In view of this, is it sufficient to consider courting *anyone* who is a believer? The answer to this is emphatically, "No"! It is not enough just to enter into courtship with a believer, nor even with a believer in assembly fellowship. There are other issues which must be the subject of careful and prayerful consideration. The Scriptural condition for marriage is that it should be "in the Lord" (1 Cor 7.39). This means that this step, with the courtship which precedes it, must be taken with a clear conviction that it is the will of the Lord. When you meet someone, and find that a mutual attraction is developing, consider whether you both have a similar interest in spiritual things and that there is agreement between you on the fundamental issues of Scripture. Have you hopes and plans for life which are compatible and which are based on a desire to know and practise the will of God? Do you both have an interest in attending assembly gatherings, or is there reluctance on the part of one to become too involved? As you gradually get to know each other better, and as you pray, you will find whether there is a basis for the friendship blossoming into courtship. This is not reducing love and courtship to a series of questions and answers where, if there are enough plus points, the conclusion is, "Yes". It is simply pointing out the issues which should be in the mind of any believer facing a friendship developing along these lines. There is no formula, but there is the need for great care.

Courting is a time of great happiness, getting to know each other better, and finding your love grow, eventually leading to engagement. Remember that engagement is not just an opportunity for a girl to obtain a fine-looking ring. To be engaged is to be promised to another and must only be entered into when a firm decision to marry has been taken before the Lord.

At this time the conduct of the believer must be carefully guarded. The world treats chastity before marriage as an unimportant thing. If two people plan to marry, they argue, what difference does a few weeks or months make? What difference does a marriage licence make? Is it really important if you anticipate marriage before the ceremony? It most certainly is! The Word of God is quite clear that a physical relationship is only permissible within marriage. Two young believers desirous of pleasing God will remain chaste until after the marriage ceremony, as anything else is designated "fornication" in Scripture. This may seem strong language but if we believe Scripture to be the Word of God we accept this as His verdict. To engage in an illicit relationship, even with one whom you plan to marry will leave a cloud over your future life. It will be something that you will never forget. It is conduct that would demand action by the assembly and, although you may seek to hide it from others, remember that it is known to God. Far better to exercise self-control and look forward to the day of marriage, with all the anticipation of entering fully into the joys, the privileges, and the responsibilities of married life, knowing that you kept yourself pure.

The marriage which you plan is much more than a physical relationship. The vows made are a public declaration of your intention to share your life together, to love each in the dark days and in the bright days, and in that love to create a home where the Lord Jesus is honoured. It also means providing for each other the spiritual, emotional, and physical support and comfort which are so necessary for a happy and godly family life.

Enjoy your courtship, respect the purity of each other, give the Lord the first place, commit your future to Him, and thus lay a good foundation for your life together.

CHAPTER 21

What about Marriage?

Entering into marriage is a major milestone in the life of a young believer. Courtship is a time of relative freedom and lack of care. You have time to plan your weekends as you wish, to attend as many meetings as is possible, and to enjoy the company of your friends without being subject to the responsibilities of running a home. After marriage things change; immediately there are tasks about the house which take up your time, there are meals to be made and washing to be done. Later, should children be born, you are no longer able to go out together, there are now others who have to be considered, money is tight and the bills seem to keep coming in relentlessly. How easy it is to find that the daily grind of life rubs the gloss from marriage. Yet marriage is for life. No believer enters it with anything else in mind. The casual approach of the world is opposed to all that the Scripture teaches. So how is it possible to preserve the warmth of your love through all the ups and downs of life?

As far as the husband is concerned he is the head of the wife (Eph 5.23). In our society, in which so called "equality" is the order of the day, it may seem strange to emphasise this truth. Holding this position does not mean that the husband acts as a dictator and domineers his wife, for his headship is "as Christ is the head of the church". It does mean that he is responsible for the well-being of his wife spiritually and, where health allows, materially. He provides leadership in the home, ensuring that the Word of God and prayer have their rightful place, and so lives that all members of the family can respect this leadership. How can this be carried out practically?

Remember that the Scriptures exhort the husband to love his wife. Love is not some tender plant which flourishes even when it is left alone. It must be nurtured. This love has to be a selfless love, "as Christ also loved the church, and gave himself for it" (Eph 5.25), and as strong as the husband's love for himself. He will, therefore, put the well-being of his wife before his own. It can be difficult for one who has only had to consider his own needs and wishes to find that those of his wife now come first. In early married life, when resources may be stretched, this will be put to the test and the husband will have ample opportunity to show his love in a very practical way by even denying himself and ensuring that provision is made for his wife.

In Colossians 3.19 the exhortation to husbands is to love their wives and "be not bitter against them". This anticipates a situation where a husband begins to feel the loss of the freedom which he remembers from his unmarried days, resulting in a feeling of bitterness against his wife, almost blaming her for the responsibilities and restrictions of married life. To arrive home from work and find a tired wife, who does not seem to have the same sparkle and attraction now that there is a home to look after, and perhaps children to care for, can create a feeling of resentment. When faced with this the husband remembers the Scripture and takes the opportunity of showing his wife that his love is as strong as ever.

The husband is also responsible for nourishing and cherishing his wife (Eph 5.29). Her well-being is in his hands and it is his prime role to provide financially for the needs of the family. There may be times when ill health and unemployment come in and some adjustment will become necessary, but where a man is fit and can obtain employment he must accept this responsibility.

We are living in an age when young married couples are urged to enter into financial commitments which are onerous. There is the need for a home, a car is the accepted norm, a house completely furnished is the order of the day, but please beware of entering into financial commitments which are beyond you. Battling to meet these can place a strain on marriage and can blight your spiritual life.

So what now of the wives? They are taught to submit themselves unto their own husbands. This does not indicate that a wife should live in fear of her husband - no spiritual husband would desire such a situation - but that she should acknowledge the fact that her husband is the head of the family. This is a responsibility which, as we have seen, the husband should fulfil in a way which earns the respect of his wife. If a little feeling of resentment comes in, remember that this relationship is only part of that greater relationship – "the head of every man is Christ; and the head of the women is the man" (1 Cor 11.3) - and is also a picture of the Headship of Christ over the church (Eph 5.23). Rather than look on this order as restrictive, consider the great honour of having a role in such a great design.

As it is the prime responsibility of the husband to provide for his family so it is the prime responsibility of the wife to manage the home. "Guide the house", and, "Give none occasion to the adversary to speak reproachfully" (1 Tim 5.14) is sound advice. The management of a home is a great responsibility and a privilege. When children come along the mother is required in the home to care for the young and to be there when needed. These early years are a time when lasting impressions are made, and a mother who orders her life to spend time with the children, teaching them, correcting them, and watching over them is fulfilling one of the most vital roles which was ever given. It is demanding, costly, without the perceived "freedom" of full time employment, and made all the more difficult by present-day pressures to sacrifice that role in furtherance of a career. Some sisters are forced by necessity to continue in employment during this time, but how much more satisfying to order your lives so that the children can have the time and attention from their mother which is so vital in their upbringing.

We all like to have someone on whom to model ourselves and spiritual wives will find such a model in 1 Peter 3.1-6. Sarah, who was a beautiful woman to look at, has left us an example of how a godly wife should live, and, as a result she is found amongst the giants of faith (Heb 11.11). True spiritual beauty is not gained by outward cosmetics, but by the adornment of spiritual character. Physical beauty fades, but this beauty increases with age.

With a home so ordered it will be possible to carry out one service for the saints which is of immeasurable value. The provision of hospitality has been used of God to great blessing. The present writer owes much to a godly family who opened their home to him when he knew almost no one in assembly fellowship. When hospitality is offered unbelievers can see how godliness is worked out in the home, young believers can meet in an environment which is profitable, older servants can be refreshed, and even strangers can be brought into touch with the gospel. In this way your home can be used of God to the blessing of many.

So strive, therefore, to make your house a home; not a place to fill with all the latest gadgets so that others might be impressed, but a place where impressions are left of the presence of God. As life goes on, and as love for each other deepens, it is an inestimable privilege to enjoy the goodness of God in making both husband and wife "heirs together of the grace of life" (1 Pet 3.7), recognising that there is an even higher relationship which is eternal and which both will share.

CHAPTER 22

Approved unto God

"Study to shew thyself approved unto God, a workman that needeth not to be ashamed, rightly dividing the word of truth" (2 Tim 2.15).

As we think about all the issues involved in living for God we would do well to consider this exhortation of Paul to Timothy. The younger man, Timothy, is being instructed by Paul to show to others the features which will enable him to exercise a ministry among the saints. "Be energetic", writes the apostle, "to show yourself approved unto God".

Note, first, that the prime desire of Timothy should be to be approved unto God, not unto men. The word "approved" indicates something that has been tried and tested. It was used when an apprentice reached the end of his apprenticeship and had to produce a piece of work which demonstrated that he was fit to be a master craftsman. This masterpiece was examined by the master, and if it passed his scrutiny it was stamped with the word "Approved". If, however, it failed to come up to standard it was stamped, "Disapproved".

With the approval of God on his work Timothy will be a workman who does not need to be ashamed, that is, a workman who does not need to cast his eyes down when the Master is scrutinising the results of his labour.

As we read these words we are moved to ask the question. How can we achieve this end? Paul gives us the answer to this in the words that follow: "rightly dividing the word of truth". To rightly divide is to handle something correctly. Thus the ploughman who ploughed a straight furrow, the housewife who cut a straight slice from the loaf, and the builder who built a straight wall, were all said to be rightly dividing. It was simply the mark of a workman who knew his trade and performed his task expertly. This could only come with patient perseverance and application to his work.

Is this not how we can be approved of God? Persevere in the reading of the Scriptures; get to know them and make them part of your being so that you can order your life and witness according to His desires. Ignorance has no value in the sight of God!

Note carefully that this happy condition will not come to pass without effort on our part. We must expend energy, time, and resources to realise this aim. God has so ordered life that nothing is achieved without effort, and there is no more worthy ambition than that of being "approved unto God".

Let us all determine to go on living for God so that we will be able to bear His gaze with dignity when His assessment of our work is made known to us.